DOVER · THRIFT · EDITIONS

Civil War Poetry

AN ANTHOLOGY

EDITED BY

PAUL NEGRI

DOVER PUBLICATIONS, INC.
Mineola, New York

DOVER THRIFT EDITIONS

GENERAL EDITOR: PAUL NEGRI

Copyright

Bibliographical Note

Civil War Poetry is a new anthology, first published by Dover Publications, Inc., in 1997.

Library of Congress Cataloging-in-Publication Data

Civil War poetry : an anthology / edited by Paul Negri.
    p.   cm. — (Dover thrift editions)
  ISBN 0-486-29883-3
    I. United States—History—Civil War, 1861–1865—Poetry. 2. American poetry—19th century. 3. War poetry, American. I. Negri, Paul. II. Series.
PS595.C55C58   1997
811'.3080358—dc21

                                           97-20645
                                              CIP

Manufactured in the United States of America
Dover Publications, Inc., 31 East 2nd Street, Mineola, N.Y. 11501

Note

THE TRIUMPHS AND TRAGEDIES of the American Civil War inspired contemporary poets to write a vast amount of verse for an avidly interested public. Replete with great causes, heroic figures, monumental battles, and legions of slain to be memorialized, the Civil War provided inexhaustible grist for the poet's mill. The quality of what that mill produced, however, varied wildly. Some poems are little better than jingoistic or sentimental doggerel; many are fairly good poems, well-suited for the occasion, if not for posterity; and some (a small number) are among the great poems of American literature.

This anthology presents a sampling of the good and the great poems written, in most cases, in the years immediately preceding, during, or immediately following the war. The roster of poets includes such major writers as Whitman, Melville, Emerson, Whittier, Lanier, Longfellow, and many more. Included, too, are poets remembered today for only a few works, some for just a single poem: Julia Ward Howe, Francis Miles Finch, Ethel Lynn Beers, Francis Orrery Ticknor, and others. Also represented are poets whose names are now forgotten, but whose works reflect with special clarity the tenor of the times or capture with peculiar vividness a particular moment in the long and terrible years of struggle.

Great figures on both sides of the conflict populate these verses. Lee, Grant, "Stonewall" Jackson, John Brown, Sheridan, Pickett, and others who fought and rode to glory are frequent subjects. So, too, are the great battles: Sumter, Gettysburg, Manassas, Seven Pines, Shiloh, Fredericksburg, Mobile Bay, and many lesser engagements as well. In some cases these battle pieces were written by war correspondents and others who witnessed the action firsthand (Henry Howard Brownell's "The Bay Fight," for example). And the war that killed over 600,000 spawned innumerable memorials to the dead, ranging in scope and tone from Ethel Lynn Beers's sentimental (and enormously popular) "'All Quiet Along the Potomac,'" on the death of a solitary sentry, to Walt Whitman's transcendent masterpiece "When Lilacs Last in the Dooryard Bloom'd," on the death of Lincoln.

The poems in this collection vary greatly in style and substance, in skill of execution, and in literary merit. But there is an essential quality that binds them all together: they are poems written by Americans caught up in the most momentous events of the nation's history. Read as part and parcel of those extraordinary times, they continue to inform and inspire us.

Contents

JULIA WARD HOWE (1819–1910). Poet, abolitionist, feminist. Her most famous poem, "Battle Hymn of the Republic," was first published in February, 1862. In April of that year it appeared set to music with the addition of the "Glory Hallelujah" chorus, which was not part of the poem as originally published.

Battle Hymn of the Republic

Mine eyes have seen the glory of the coming of the Lord:
He is trampling out the vintage where the grapes of wrath are stored;
He hath loosed the fateful lightning of his terrible swift sword:
    His truth is marching on.

I have seen Him in the watch-fires of a hundred circling camps;
They have builded Him an altar in the evening dews and damps:
I can read his righteous sentence by the dim and flaring lamps.
    His day is marching on.

I have read a fiery gospel, writ in burnished rows of steel:
"As ye deal with my contemners, so with you my grace shall deal;
Let the Hero, born of woman, crush the serpent with his heel,
    Since God is marching on."

He has sounded forth the trumpet that shall never call retreat;
He is sifting out the hearts of men before his judgment-seat:
Oh! be swift, my soul, to answer Him! be jubilant, my feet!
    Our God is marching on.

In the beauty of the lilies Christ was born across the sea,
With a glory in his bosom that transfigures you and me:
As He died to make men holy, let us die to make men free,
    While God is marching on.

Pardon

John Wilkes Booth

Pains the sharp sentence the heart in whose wrath it was uttered,
　　　Now thou art cold;
Vengeance, the headlong, and Justice, with purpose close muttered,
　　　Loosen their hold.

Death brings atonement; he did that whereof ye accuse him—
　　　Murder accurst;
But from that crisis of crime in which Satan did lose him,
　　　Suffered the worst.

Harshly the red dawn arose on a deed of his doing,
　　　Never to mend;
But harsher days he wore out in the bitter pursuing
　　　And the wild end.

So lift the pale flag of truce, wrap those mysteries round him,
　　　In whose avail
Madness that moved, and the swift retribution that found him,
　　　Falter and fail.

So the soft purples that quiet the heavens with mourning,
　　　Willing to fall,
Lend him one fold, his illustrious victim adorning
　　　With wider pall.

Back to the cross, where the Saviour uplifted in dying
　　　Bade all souls live,
Turns the reft bosom of Nature, his mother, low sighing,
　　　Greatest, forgive!

Robert E. Lee

A gallant foeman in the fight,
　A brother when the fight was o'er,
The hand that led the host with might
　The blessed torch of learning bore.

Thought may the minds of men divide,
Love makes the heart of nations one,
And so, thy soldier grave beside,
We honor thee, Virginia's son.

HENRY TIMROD (1829–1867). Major lyric poet of the pre-War South. Called the "Poet Laureate of the Confederacy," he served briefly in the Confederate army in 1862, but was discharged due to ill health.

Ethnogenesis

Written during the meeting of the first Southern Congress,
at Montgomery, February, 1861.

I.

Hath not the morning dawned with added light?
And will not evening call another star
Out of the infinite regions of the night,
To mark this day in Heaven? At last, we are
A nation among nations; and the world
Shall soon behold in many a distant port
    Another Flag unfurled!
Now, come what may, whose favor need we court?
And, under God, whose thunder need we fear?
    Thank Him who placed us here
Beneath so kind a sky—the very sun
Takes part with us; and on our errands run
All breezes of the ocean; dew and rain
Do noiseless battle for us; and the Year,
And all the gentle daughters in her train,
March in our ranks, and in our service wield
    Long spears of golden grain!
A yellow blossom as her fairy shield,
June flings her azure banner to the wind,
    While in the order of their birth
Her sisters pass, and many an ample field
Grows white beneath their steps, till now, behold
    Its endless sheets unfold

THE SNOW OF SOUTHERN SUMMERS! Let the earth
Rejoice! beneath those fleeces soft and warm
      Our happy land shall sleep
      In a repose as deep
   As if we lay intrenched behind
Whole leagues of Russian ice and Arctic storm!

II.

And what if, mad with wrongs themselves have wrought,
      In their own treachery caught,
      By their own fears made bold,
      And leagued with him of old,
Who long since in the limits of the North
Set up his evil throne, and warred with God—
What if, both mad and blinded in their rage,
Our foes should fling us down their mortal gage,
And with a hostile step profane our sod!
We shall not shrink, my brothers, but go forth
To meet them, marshalled by the Lord of Hosts,
And overshadowed by the mighty ghosts
Of Moultrie and of Eutaw—who shall foil
Auxiliars such as these? Nor these alone,
      But every stock and stone
      Shall help us: but the very soil,
And all the generous wealth it gives to toil,
And all for which we love our noble land,
Shall fight beside, and through us, sea and strand,
      The heart of woman, and her hand,
Tree, fruit, and flower, and every influence,
      Gentle, or grave, or grand;
The winds in our defence
Shall seem to blow; to us the hills shall lend
      Their firmness and their calm;
And in our stiffened sinews we shall blend
      The strength of pine and palm!

III.

Nor would we shun the battle-ground,
      Though weak as we are strong;

Call up the clashing elements around,
    And test the right and wrong!
On one side, creeds that dare to teach
What Christ and Paul refrained to preach;
Codes built upon a broken pledge,
And Charity that whets a poniard's edge;
Fair schemes that leave the neighboring poor
To starve and shiver at the schemer's door,
While in the world's most liberal ranks enrolled,
He turns some vast philanthropy to gold;
Religion, taking every mortal form
But that a pure and Christian faith makes warm,
Where not to vile fanatic passion urged,
Or not in vague philosophies submerged,
Repulsive with all Pharisaic leaven,
And making laws to stay the laws of Heaven!
And on the other, scorn of sordid gain,
Unblemished honor, truth without a stain,
Faith, justice, reverence, charitable wealth,
And, for the poor and humble, laws which give,
Not the mean right to buy the right to live,
    But life, and home, and health!
To doubt the end were want of trust in God,
    Who, if he has decreed
  That we must pass a redder sea
Than that which rang to Miriam's holy glee,
    Will surely raise at need
    A Moses with his rod!

IV.

But let our fears—if fears we have—be still,
And turn us to the future! Could we climb
Some mighty Alp, and view the coming time,
We should indeed behold a sight to fill
    Our eyes with happy tears!
Not for the glories which a hundred years
Shall bring us; not for lands from sea to sea,
And wealth, and power, and peace, though these shall be;

But for the distant peoples we shall bless,
And the hushed murmurs of a world's distress:
For, to give labor to the poor,
    The whole sad plant o'er,
And save from want and crime the humblest door,
Is one among the many ends for which
    God makes us great and rich!
The hour perchance is not yet wholly ripe
When all shall own it, but the type
Whereby we shall be known in every land
Is that vast gulf which laves our Southern strand,
And through the cold, untempered ocean pours
Its genial streams, that far off Arctic shores
May sometimes catch upon the softened breeze
Strange tropic warmth and hints of summer seas.

Charleston

Calm as that second summer which precedes
    The first fall of the snow,
In the broad sunlight of heroic deeds,
    The city bides the foe.

As yet, behind their ramparts, stern and proud,
    Her bolted thunders sleep—
Dark Sumter, like a battlemented cloud,
    Looms o'er the solemn deep.

No Calpe frowns from lofty cliff or scaur
    To guard the holy strand;
But Moultrie holds in leash her dogs of war
    Above the level sand.

And down the dunes a thousand guns lie couched,
    Unseen, beside the flood—
Like tigers in some Orient jungle crouched,
    That wait and watch for blood.

Meanwhile, through streets still echoing with trade,
   Walk grave and thoughtful men,
Whose hands may one day wield the patriot's blade
   As lightly as the pen.

And maidens, with such eyes as would grow dim
   Over a bleeding hound,
Seem each one to have caught the strength of him
   Whose sword she sadly bound.

Thus girt without and garrisoned at home,
   Day patient following day,
Old Charleston looks from roof and spire and dome,
   Across her tranquil bay.

Ships, through a hundred foes, from Saxon lands
   And spicy Indian ports,
Bring Saxon steel and iron to her hands,
   And summer to her courts.

But still, along yon dim Atlantic line,
   The only hostile smoke
Creeps like a harmless mist above the brine,
   From some frail floating oak.

Shall the spring dawn, and she, still clad in smiles,
   And with an unscathed brow,
Rest in the strong arms of her palm-crowned isles,
   As fair and free as now?

We know not; in the temple of the Fates
   God has inscribed her doom:
And, all untroubled in her faith, she waits
   The triumph or the tomb.

A Cry to Arms

Ho, woodsmen of the mountain side!
   Ho, dwellers in the vales!

Ho, ye who by the chafing tide
   Have roughened in the gales!
Leave barn and byre, leave kin and cot,
   Lay by the bloodless spade;
Let desk and case and counter rot,
   And burn your books of trade!

The despot roves your fairest lands;
   And till he flies or fears,
You fields must grow but armed bands,
   Your sheaves be sheaves of spears!
Give up to mildew and to rust
   The useless tools of gain,
And feed your country's sacred dust
   With floods of crimson rain!

Come with the weapons at your call—
   With musket, pike, or knife;
He wields the deadliest blade of all
   Who lightest holds his life.
The arm that drives its unbought blows
   With all a patriot's scorn,
Might brain a tyrant with a rose
   Or stab him with a thorn.

Does any falter? Let him turn
   To some brave maiden's eyes,
And catch the holy fires that burn
   In those sublunar skies.
Oh, could you like your women feel,
   And in their spirit march,
A day might see your lines of steel
   Beneath the victor's arch!

What hope, O God! would not grow warm
   When thoughts like these give cheer?
The lily calmly braves the storm,
   And shall the palm tree fear?
No! rather let its branches court
   The rack that sweeps the plain;
And from the lily's regal port
   Learn how to breast the strain.

Ho, woodsmen of the mountain side!
  Ho, dwellers in the vales!
Ho, ye who by the roaring tide
  Have roughened in the gales!
Come, flocking gayly to the fight,
  From forest, hill, and lake;
We battle for our country's right,
  And for the lily's sake!

Carolina

The despot treads thy sacred sands,
Thy pines give shelter to his bands,
Thy sons stand by with idle hands,
    Carolina!
He breathes at ease thy airs of balm,
He scorns the lances of thy palm;
Oh! who shall break thy craven calm,
    Carolina!
Thy ancient fame is growing dim,
A spot is on thy garment's rim;
Give to the winds thy battle-hymn,
    Carolina!

Call on thy children of the hill,
Wake swamp and river, coast and rill,
Rouse all thy strength and all thy skill,
    Carolina!
Cite wealth and science, trade and art,
Touch with thy fire the cautious mart,
And pour thee through the people's heart,
    Carolina!
Till even the coward spurns his fears,
And all thy fields, and fens, and meres
Shall bristle like thy palm with spears,
    Carolina!

I hear a murmur as of waves
That grope their way through sunless caves,
Like bodies struggling in their graves,
    Carolina!

And now it deepens; slow and grand
It swells, as, rolling to the land,
An ocean broke upon thy strand,
   Carolina!
Shout! Let it reach the startled Huns!
And roar with all thy festal guns!
It is the answer of thy sons,
   Carolina!

Ode at Magnolia Cemetery

Sung on the occasion of decorating the graves of the Confederate dead,
at Magnolia Cemetery, Charleston, on Memorial Day, April, 1867.

Sleep sweetly in your humble graves,
 Sleep, martyrs of a fallen cause;
Though yet no marble column craves
 The pilgrim here to pause.

In seeds of laurel in the earth
 The blossom of your fame is blown,
And somewhere, waiting for its birth,
 The shaft is in the stone!
Meanwhile, behalf the tardy years
 Which keep in trust your storied tombs,
Behold! your sisters bring their tears,
 And these memorial blooms.

Small tributes! but your shades will smile
 More proudly on these wreaths to-day,
Than when some cannon-moulded pile
 Shall overlook this bay.

Stoop, angels, hither from the skies!
 There is no holier spot of ground
Than where defeated valor lies,
 By mourning beauty crowned.

JAMES SLOAN GIBBONS (1810–1892). Abolitionist. Gibbons's poem was written in response to Lincoln's call in July 1862 for 300,000 volunteers to enlist in the Union army. The poem was quickly set to music by several composers, the most famous version being by L. O. Emerson.

Three Hundred Thousand More

We are coming, Father Abraham, three hundred thousand more,
From Mississippi's winding stream and from New England's shore;
We leave our ploughs and workshops, our wives and children dear,
With hearts too full for utterance, with but a silent tear;
We dare not look behind us, but steadfastly before:
We are coming, Father Abraham, three hundred thousand more!

If you look across the hill tops that meet the northern sky,
Long moving lines of rising dust your vision may descry;
And now the wind, an instant, tears the cloudy veil aside,
And floats aloft our spangled flag in glory and in pride,
And bayonets in the sunlight gleam, and bands brave music pour:
We are coming, Father Abraham, three hundred thousand more!

If you look all up our valleys where the growing harvests shine,
You may see our sturdy farmer boys fast forming into line;
And children from their mother's knees are pulling at the weeds,
And learning how to reap and sow against their country's needs;
And a farewell group stands weeping at every cottage door:
We are coming, Father Abraham, three hundred thousand more!

You have called us, and we're coming, by Richmond's bloody tide
To lay us down, for Freedom's sake, our brothers' bones beside,
Or from foul treason's savage grasp to wrench the murderous blade,
And in the face of foreign foes its fragments to parade.
Six hundred thousand loyal men and true have gone before:
We are coming, Father Abraham, three hundred thousand more!

JAMES RYDER RANDALL (1839–1908). Poet and journalist. "My Maryland," published in May 1861, appeared later in the year set to the music of "O Tannenbaum, O Tannenbaum!" and came to be known as the "Marseillaise of the Confederate cause."

My Maryland

The despot's heel is on thy shore,
    Maryland!
His torch is at thy temple door,
    Maryland!
Avenge the patriotic gore
That flecked the streets of Baltimore,
And be the battle queen of yore,
    Maryland, my Maryland!

Hark to an exiled son's appeal,
    Maryland!
My Mother State, to thee I kneel,
    Maryland!
For life and death, for woe and weal,
Thy peerless chivalry reveal,
And gird thy beauteous limbs with steel,
    Maryland, my Maryland!

Thou wilt not cower in the dust,
    Maryland!
Thy beaming sword shall never rust,
    Maryland!
Remember Carroll's sacred trust,
Remember Howard's warlike thrust,
And all thy slumberers with the just,
    Maryland, my Maryland!

Come! 't is the red dawn of the day,
    Maryland!
Come with thy panoplied array,
    Maryland!
With Ringgold's spirit for the fray,
With Watson's blood at Monterey,

With fearless Lowe and dashing May,
    Maryland, my Maryland!
Dear Mother, burst the tyrant's chain,
    Maryland!
Virginia should not call in vain,
    Maryland!
She meets her sisters on the plain—
"*Sic semper!*" 't is the proud refrain
That baffles minions back amain,
    Maryland!
Arise in majesty again,
    Maryland, my Maryland!

Come! for thy shield is bright and strong,
    Maryland!
Come! for thy dalliance does thee wrong,
    Maryland!
Come to thine own heroic throng
Stalking with Liberty along,
And chant thy dauntless slogan song,
    Maryland, my Maryland!

I see the blush upon thy cheek,
    Maryland!
For thou wast ever bravely meek,
    Maryland!
But lo! there surges forth a shriek,
From hill to hill, from creek to creek,
Potomac calls to Chesapeake,
    Maryland, my Maryland!

Thou wilt not yield the Vandal toll,
    Maryland!
Thou wilt not crook to his control,
    Maryland!
Better the fire upon thee roll,
Better the shot, the blade, the bowl,
Than crucifixion of the soul,
    Maryland, my Maryland!

I hear the distant thunder hum,
    Maryland!
The Old Line's bugle, fife, and drum,
    Maryland!
She is not dead, nor deaf, nor dumb;
Huzza! she spurns the Northern scum!
She breathes! She burns! She'll come! She'll come!
    Maryland, my Maryland!

RALPH WALDO EMERSON (1803–1882). Essayist and poet. "Boston Hymn" was recited by Emerson at a public reading on the day that the Emancipation Proclamation took effect, January 1, 1863.

Boston Hymn

The word of the Lord by night
    To the watching Pilgrims came,
As they sat by the seaside,
    And filled their hearts with flame.

God said, I am tired of kings,
    I suffer them no more;
Up to my ear the morning brings
    The outrage of the poor.

Think ye I made this ball
    A field of havoc and war,
Where tyrants great and tyrants small
    Might harry the weak and poor?

My angel—his name is Freedom—
    Choose him to be your king;
He shall cut pathways east and west,
    And fend you with his wing.

Lo! I uncover the land,
    Which I hid of old time in the West,
As the sculptor uncovers the statue
    When he has wrought his best;

I show Columbia, of the rocks
   Which dip their foot in the seas,
And soar to the air borne flocks
   Of clouds and the boreal fleece.

I will divide my goods;
   Call in the wretch and slave;
None shall rule but the humble,
   And none but Toil shall have.

I will have never a noble,
   No lineage counted great;
Fishers and choppers and ploughmen
   Shall constitute a state.

Go, cut down trees in the forest
   And trim the straightest boughs;
Cut down trees in the forest
   And build me a wooden house.

Call the people together,
   The young men and the sires,
The digger in the harvest field,
   Hireling and him that hires;

And here in a pine state house
   They shall choose men to rule
In every needful faculty,
   In church and state and school.

Lo, now! if these poor men
   Can govern the land and sea,
And make just laws below the sun,
   As planets faithful be.

And ye shall succor men;
   'T is nobleness to serve;
Help them who cannot help again:
   Beware from right to swerve.

I break your bonds and masterships,
   And I unchain the slave:

Free be his heart and hand henceforth
   As wind and wandering wave.

I cause from every creature
   His proper good to flow;
As much as he is and doeth,
   So much he shall bestow.

But, laying hands on another,
   To coin his labor and sweat,
He goes in pawn to his victim
   For eternal years in debt.

Today unbind the captive,
   So only are ye unbound;
Lift up a people from the dust,
   Trump of their rescue, sound!

Pay ransom to the owner
   And fill the bag to the brim.
Who is the owner? The slave is owner
   And ever was. Pay him.

O North! give him beauty for rags,
   And honor, O South! for his shame;
Nevada! coin thy golden crags
   With Freedom's image and name.

Up! and the dusky race
   That sat in darkness long—
Be swift their feet as antelopes,
   And as behemoth strong.

Come, East and West and North,
   By races, as snowflakes,
And carry my purpose forth,
   Which neither halts nor shakes.

My will fulfilled shall be,
   For, in daylight or in dark,
My thunderbolt has eyes to see
   His way home to the mark.

JOHN GREENLEAF WHITTIER (1807–1892). A Quaker, Whittier was an ardent abolitionist and one of the most prolific and popular poets of his time. "Barbara Frietchie" is one of the best-known and best-loved American poems.

Brown of Ossawatomie

John Brown of Ossawatomie spake on his dying day:
"I will not have to shrive my soul a priest in Slavery's pay.
But let some poor slave mother whom I have striven to free,
With her children, from the gallows stair put up a prayer for me!"

John Brown of Ossawatomie, they led him out to die;
And lo! a poor slave mother with her little child pressed nigh.
Then the bold, blue eye grew tender, and the old harsh face grew mild,
As he stooped between the jeering ranks and kissed the negro's child!

The shadows of his stormy life that moment fell apart;
And they who blamed the bloody hand forgave the loving heart.
That kiss from all its guilty means redeemed the good intent,
And round the grisly fighter's hair the martyr's aureole bent!

Perish with him the folly that seeks through evil good!
Long live the generous purpose unstained with human blood!
Not the raid of midnight terror, but the thought which underlies;
Not the borderer's pride of daring, but the Christian's sacrifice.

Nevermore may yon Blue Ridges the Northern rifle hear,
Nor see the light of blazing homes flash on the negro's spear.
But let the free winged angel Truth their guarded passes scale,
To teach that right is more than might, and justice more than mail!

So vainly shall Virginia set her battle in array;
In vain her trampling squadrons knead the winter snow with clay.
She may strike the pouncing eagle, but she dares not harm the dove;
And every gate she bars to Hate shall open wide to Love!

A Word for the Hour

The firmament breaks up. In black eclipse
Light after light goes out. One evil star,
Luridly glaring through the smoke of war,

As in the dream of the Apocalypse,
Drags others down. Let us not weakly weep
Nor rashly threaten. Give us grace to keep
Our faith and patience; wherefore should we leap
On one hand into fratricidal fight,
Or, on the other, yield eternal right,
Frame lies of law, and good and ill confound?
What fear we? Safe on freedom's vantage ground
Our feet are planted: let us there remain
In unrevengeful calm, no means untried
Which truth can sanction, no just claim denied,
The sad spectators of a suicide!
They break the links of Union: shall we light
The fires of hell to weld anew the chain
On that red anvil where each blow is pain?
Draw we not even now a freer breath,
As from our shoulders falls a load of death
Loathsome as that the Tuscan's victim bore
When keen with life to a dead horror bound?
Why take we up the accursed thing again?
Pity, forgive, but urge them back no more
Who, drunk with passion, flaunt disunion's rag
With its vile reptile-blazon. Let us press
The golden cluster on our brave old flag
In closer union, and, if numbering less,
Brighter shall shine the stars which still remain.

The Battle Autumn of 1862

The flags of war like storm birds fly,
    The charging trumpets blow;
Yet rolls no thunder in the sky,
    No earthquake strives below.

And, calm and patient, Nature keeps
    Her ancient promise well,
Though o'er her bloom and greenness sweeps
    The battle's breath of hell.

And still she walks in golden hours
    Through harvest happy farms,
And still she wears her fruits and flowers
    Like jewels on her arms.

What mean the gladness of the plain,
    This joy of eve and morn,
The mirth that shakes the beard of grain
    And yellow locks of corn?

Ah! eyes may well be full of tears,
    And hearts with hate are hot;
But even paced come round the years,
    And Nature changes not.

She meets with smiles our bitter grief,
    With songs our groans of pain;
She mocks with tint of flower and leaf
    The war field's crimson stain.

Still, in the cannon's pause, we hear
    Her sweet thanksgiving psalm;
Too near to God for doubt or fear,
    She shares the eternal calm.

She knows the seed lies safe below
    The fires that blast and burn;
For all the tears of blood we sow
    She waits the rich return.

She sees with clearer eye than ours
    The good of suffering born—
The hearts that blossom like her flowers,
    And ripen like her corn.

Oh, give to us, in times like these,
    The vision of her eyes;
And make her fields and fruited trees
    Our golden prophecies!

Oh, give to us her finer ear!
    Above this stormy din,
We too would hear the bells of cheer
    Ring peace and freedom in.

"Ein feste Burg ist unser Gott"

We wait beneath the furnace blast
    The pangs of transformation;
Not painlessly doth God recast
    And mould anew the nation.
        Hot burns the fire
        Where wrongs expire;
        Nor spares the hand
        That from the land
    Uproots the ancient evil.

The hand breadth cloud the sages feared
    Its bloody rain is dropping;
The poison plant the fathers spared
    All else is overtopping.
        East, West, South, North,
        It curses the earth;
        All justice dies,
        And fraud and lies
    Live only in its shadow.

What gives the wheat field blades of steel?
    What points the rebel cannon?
What sets the roaring rabble's heel
    On the old star-spangled pennon?
        What breaks the oath
        Of the men o' the South?
        What whets the knife
        For the Union's life?—
    Hark to the answer: Slavery!

Then waste no blows on lesser foes
    In strife unworthy freemen.

God lifts today the veil, and shows
  The features of the demon!
    O North and South,
    Its victims both,
    Can ye not cry,
    "Let slavery die!"
  And union find in freedom?

What though the cast out spirit tear
  The nation in his going?
We who have shared the guilt must share
  The pang of his o'erthrowing!
    Whate'er the loss,
    Whate'er the cross,
    Shall they complain
    Of present pain
  Who trust in God's hereafter?

For who that leans on His right arm
  Was ever yet forsaken?
What righteous cause can suffer harm
  If He its part has taken?
    Though wild and loud,
    And dark the cloud,
    Behind its folds
    His hand upholds
  The calm sky of tomorrow!

Above the maddening cry for blood,
  Above the wild war drumming,
Let Freedom's voice be heard, with good
  The evil overcoming.
    Give prayer and purse
    To stay the Curse
    Whose wrong we share,
    Whose shame we bear,
  Whose end shall gladden Heaven!

In vain the bells of war shall ring
  Of triumphs and revenges,

While still is spared the evil thing
   That severs and estranges.
      But blest the ear
      That yet shall hear
      The jubilant bell
      That rings the knell
Of Slavery forever!

Then let the selfish lip be dumb,
   And hushed the breath of sighing;
Before the joy of peace must come
   The pains of purifying.
      God give us grace
      Each in his place
      To bear his lot,
      And, murmuring not,
Endure and wait and labor!

Laus Deo!

On hearing the bells ring on the passage of the
constitutional amendment abolishing slavery.

      It is done!
   Clang of bell and roar of gun
  Send the tidings up and down.
    How the belfries rock and reel!
    How the great guns, peal on peal,
Fling the joy from town to town!

      Ring, O bells!
   Every stroke exulting tells
Of the burial hour of crime.
    Loud and long, that all may hear,
    Ring for every listening ear
Of Eternity and Time!

      Let us kneel:
   God's own voice is in that peal,

And this spot is holy ground.
 Lord, forgive us! What are we,
 That our eyes this glory see,
That our ears have heard the sound!

  For the Lord
 On the whirlwind is abroad;
In the earthquake He has spoken;
 He has smitten with His thunder
 The iron walls asunder,
And the gates of brass are broken!

  Loud and long
 Lift the old exulting song;
Sing with Miriam by the sea,
 He has cast the mighty down;
 Horse and rider sink and drown;
"He hath triumphed gloriously!"

  Did we dare,
 In our agony of prayer,
Ask for more than He has done?
 When was ever His right hand
 Over any time or land
Stretched as now beneath the sun?

  How they pale,
 Ancient myth and song and tale,
In this wonder of our days,
 When the cruel rod of war
 Blossoms white with righteous law
And the wrath of man is praise!

  Blotted out!
 All within and all about
Shall a fresher life begin;
 Freer breathe the universe
 As it rolls its heavy curse
On the dead and buried sin!

It is done!
In the circuit of the sun
Shall the sound thereof go forth.
It shall bid the sad rejoice,
It shall give the dumb a voice,
It shall belt with joy the earth!

Ring and swing,
Bells of joy! On morning's wing
Send the song of praise abroad!
With a sound of broken chains
Tell the nations that He reigns,
Who alone is Lord and God!

Barbara Frietchie

Up from the meadows rich with corn,
Clear in the cool September morn,

The clustered spires of Frederick stand
Green-walled by the hills of Maryland.

Round about them orchards sweep,
Apple and peach tree fruited deep,

Fair as the garden of the Lord
To the eyes of the famished rebel horde,

On that pleasant morn of the early fall
When Lee marched over the mountain-wall;

Over the mountains winding down,
Horse and foot, into Frederick town.

Forty flags with their silver stars,
Forty flags with their crimson bars,

Flapped in the morning wind: the sun
Of noon looked down, and saw not one.

Up rose old Barbara Frietchie then,
Bowed with her fourscore years and ten;

Bravest of all in Frederick town,
She took up the flag the men hauled down;

In her attic window the staff she set,
To show that one heart was loyal yet.

Up the street came the rebel tread,
Stonewall Jackson riding ahead.

Under his slouched hat left and right
He glanced; the old flag met his sight.

"Halt!"—the dust-brown ranks stood fast.
"Fire!"— out blazed the rifle-blast.

It shivered the window, pane and sash;
It rent the banner with seam and gash.

Quick, as it fell, from the broken staff
Dame Barbara snatched the silken scarf.

She leaned far out on the window sill,
And shook it forth with a royal will.

"Shoot, if you must, this old gray head,
But spare your country's flag," she said.

A shade of sadness, a blush of shame,
Over the face of the leader came;

The nobler nature within him stirred
To life at that woman's deed and word;

"Who touches a hair of yon gray head
Dies like a dog! March on!" he said.

All day long through Frederick street
Sounded the tread of marching feet:

All day long that free flag tost
Over the heads of the rebel host.

Ever its torn folds rose and fell
On the loyal winds that loved it well;

And through the hill-gaps sunset light
Shone over it with a warm good night.

Barbara Frietchie's work is o'er,
And the Rebel rides on his raids no more.

Honor to her! and let a tear
Fall, for her sake, on Stonewall's bier.

Over Barbara Frietchie's grave,
Flag of Freedom and Union, wave!

Peace and order and beauty draw
Round thy symbol of light and law;

And ever the stars above look down
On thy stars below in Frederick town!

WILLIAM CULLEN BRYANT (1794–1878). Poet and journalist. Author of "Thanatopsis" and "To a Waterfowl," Bryant was a strong supporter of the abolitionist cause.

The Death of Slavery

O thou great Wrong, that, through the slow-paced years,
    Didst hold thy millions fettered, and didst wield
    The scourge that drove the laborer to the field,
And turn a stony gaze on human tears,
            Thy cruel reign is o'er;
            Thy bondmen crouch no more
In terror at the menace of thine eye;
    For He who marks the bounds of guilty power,
Long-suffering, hath heard the captive's cry,
    And touched his shackles at the appointed hour,

And lo! they fall, and he whose limbs they galled
Stands in his native manhood, disenthralled.

A shout of joy from the redeemed is sent;
   Ten thousand hamlets swell the hymn of thanks;
   Our rivers roll exulting, and their banks
Send up hosannas to the firmament!
               Fields where the bondman's toil
               No more shall trench the soil,
Seem now to bask in a serener day;
   The meadow-birds sing sweeter, and the airs
Of heaven with more caressing softness play,
   Welcoming man to liberty like theirs.
A glory clothes the land from sea to sea,
For the great land and all its coasts are free.

Within that land wert thou enthroned of late,
   And they by whom the nation's laws were made,
   And they who filled its judgment-seats obeyed
Thy mandate, rigid as the will of Fate.
           Fierce men at thy right hand,
           With gesture of command,
Gave forth the word that none might dare gainsay;
   And grave and reverend ones, who loved thee not,
Shrank from thy presence, and in blank dismay
   Choked down, unuttered, the rebellious thought;
While meaner cowards, mingling with thy train,
Proved, from the book of God, thy right to reign.

Great as thou wert, and feared from shore to shore,
   The wrath of Heaven o'ertook thee in thy pride;
   Thou sitt'st a ghastly shadow; by thy side
Thy once strong arms hang nerveless evermore.
          And they who quailed but now
          Before thy lowering brow,
Devote thy memory to scorn and shame,
   And scoff at the pale, powerless thing thou art.
And they who ruled in thine imperial name,
   Subdued, and standing sullenly apart,
Scowl at the hands that overthrew thy reign,
And shattered at a blow the prisoner's chain.

Well was thy doom deserved; thou didst not spare
   Life's tenderest ties, but cruelly didst part
   Husband and wife, and from the mother's heart
Didst wrest her children, deaf to shriek and prayer;
           Thy inner lair became
           The haunt of guilty shame;
Thy lash dropped blood; the murderer, at thy side,
   Showed his red hands, nor feared the vengeance due
Thou didst sow earth with crimes, and, far and wide,
   A harvest of uncounted miseries grew,
Until the measure of thy sins at last
Was full, and then the avenging bolt was cast!

Go now, accursed of God, and take thy place
   With hateful memories of the elder time,
   With many a wasting plague, and nameless crime,
And bloody war that thinned the human race;
           With the Black Death, whose way
           Through wailing cities lay,
Worship of Moloch, tyrannies that built
   The Pyramids, and cruel creeds that taught
To avenge a fancied guilt by deeper guilt—
   Death at the stake to those that held them not.
Lo! the foul phantoms, silent in the gloom
Of the flown ages, part to yield thee room.

I see the better years that hasten by
   Carry thee back into that shadowy past,
   Where, in the dusty spaces, void and vast,
The graves of those whom thou hast murdered lie.
           The slave-pen, through whose door
           Thy victims pass no more,
Is there, and there shall the grim block remain
   At which the slave was sold; while at thy feet
Scourges and engines of restraint and pain
   Moulder and rust by thine eternal seat.
There, mid the symbols that proclaim thy crimes,
Dwell thou, a warning to the coming times.

Abraham Lincoln

Oh, slow to smite and swift to spare,
    Gentle and merciful and just!
Who, in the fear of God, didst bear
    The sword of power, a nation's trust!

In sorrow by thy bier we stand,
    Amid the awe that hushes all,
And speak the anguish of a land
    That shook with horror at thy fall.

Thy task is done; the bound are free:
    We bear thee to an honored grave,
Whose proudest monument shall be
    The broken fetters of the slave.

Pure was thy life; its bloody close
    Hath placed thee with the sons of light,
Among the noble host of those
    Who perished in the cause of Right.

ETHEL LYNN BEERS (1827–1879). Poet and writer. "'All Quiet Along the Potomac,'" first published in 1861 under the title "The Picket Guard," is among the most famous of Civil War poems.

"All Quiet Along the Potomac"

"All quiet along the Potomac," they say,
    "Except now and then a stray picket
Is shot, as he walks on his beat to and fro,
    By a rifleman hid in the thicket.
'T is nothing: a private or two, now and then,
    Will not count in the news of the battle;
Not an officer lost—only one of the men,
    Moaning out, all alone, the death rattle."

All quiet along the Potomac tonight,
    Where the soldiers lie peacefully dreaming;

Their tents in the rays of the clear autumn moon,
    Or the light of the watch-fire, are gleaming.
A tremulous sigh of the gentle night-wind
    Through the forest leaves softly is creeping,
While the stars up above, with their glittering eyes,
    Keep guard, for the army is sleeping.

There's only the sound of the lone sentry's tread
    As he tramps from the rock to the fountain,
And thinks of the two in the low trundle-bed
    Far away in the cot on the mountain.
His musket falls slack; his face, dark and grim,
    Grows gentle with memories tender,
As he mutters a prayer for the children asleep—
    For their mother—may Heaven defend her!

The moon seems to shine just as brightly as then,
    That night, when the love yet unspoken
Leaped up to his lips—when low-murmured vows
    Were pledged to be ever unbroken.
Then drawing his sleeve roughly over his eyes,
    He dashes off tears that are welling,
And gathers his gun closer up to its place
    As if to keep down the heart-swelling.

He passes the fountain, the blasted pine-tree;
    The footstep is lagging and weary;
Yet onward he goes, through the broad belt of light,
    Towards the shade of the forest so dreary.
Hark! was it the night-wind that rustled the leaves?
    Was it moonlight so wondrously flashing?
It looked like a rifle . . . "Ha! Mary, good by!"
    The red life-blood is ebbing and plashing.

All quiet along the Potomac tonight—
    No sound save the rush of the river,
While soft falls the dew on the face of the dead—
    The picket's off duty forever!

SIDNEY LANIER (1842–1881). Lanier served in the Confederate army and saw action in major engagements. "Stonewall" Jackson, memorialized in poems by Lanier and many others, was accidentally shot and killed by Confederate pickets at Chancellorsville on May 2, 1863.

The Dying Words of Stonewall Jackson

"Order A. P. Hill to prepare for battle."
"Tell Major Hawks to advance the commissary train."
"Let us cross the river and rest in the shade."*

The stars of Night contain the glittering Day
And rain his glory down with sweeter grace
Upon the dark World's grand, enchanted face—
　　All loth to turn away.

And so the Day, about to yield his breath,
Utters the stars unto the listening Night,
To stand for burning fare-thee-wells of light
　　Said on the verge of death.

O hero life that lit us like the sun!
O hero words that glittered like the stars
And stood and shone above the gloomy wars
　　When the hero life was done!

The phantoms of a battle came to dwell
I' the fitful vision of his dying eyes—
Yet even in battle dreams, he sends supplies
　　To those he loved so well.

His army stands in battle line arrayed:
His couriers fly: all's done: now God decide!
—And not till then saw he the Other Side
　　Or would accept the shade.

Thou Land whose sun is gone, thy stars remain!
Still shine the words that miniature his deeds.
O thrice-beloved, where'er thy great heart bleeds,
　　Solace hast thou for pain!

* Jackson's dying words, spoken in delirium.

THOMAS BAILEY ALDRICH (1836–1907). Poet and novelist. From the
outbreak of the Civil War to 1862, he was war correspondent of the New York
Tribune. He was editor of the *Atlantic Monthly* from 1881 to 1890.

Fredericksburg

The increasing moonlight drifts across my bed,
And on the churchyard by the road, I know
It falls as white and noiselessly as snow. . . .
'T was such a night two weary summers fled;
The stars, as now, were waning overhead.
Listen! Again the shrill-lipped bugles blow
Where the swift currents of the river flow
Past Fredericksburg; far off the heavens are red
With sudden conflagration: on yon height,
Linstock in hand, the gunners hold their breath;
A signal rocket pierces the dense night,
Flings its spent stars upon the town beneath:
Hark!—the artillery massing on the right,
Hark!—the black squadrons wheeling down to Death!

By the Potomac

The soft new grass is creeping o'er the graves
By the Potomac; and the crisp ground flower
Tilts its blue cup to catch the passing shower;
The pine cone ripens, and the long moss waves
Its tangled gonfalons above our braves.
Hark, what a burst of music from yon bower!—
The Southern nightingale that hour by hour
In its melodious summer madness raves.
Ah, with what delicate touches of her hand,
With what sweet voice of bird and rivulet
And drowsy murmur of the rustling leaf
Would Nature soothe us, bidding us forget
The awful crime of this distracted land
And all our heavy heritage of grief.

FRANCIS ORRERY TICKNOR (1822–1874). Poet and physician. The "Little Giffen" of his famous poem was a young Confederate soldier severely wounded at the battle of Murfreesboro. He was nursed back to health by Dr. Ticknor, only to be killed in a later battle.

Little Giffen

Out of the focal and foremost fire,
Out of the hospital walls as dire,
Smitten of grape shot and gangrene
(Eighteenth battle and *he* sixteen)—
Spectre such as you seldom see,
Little Giffen of Tennessee.

"Take him—and welcome!" the surgeons said,
"Little the doctor can help the dead!"
So we took him and brought him where
The balm was sweet on the summer air;
And we laid him down on a wholesome bed—
Utter Lazarus, heel to head!

And we watched the war with bated breath—
Skeleton Boy against skeleton Death.
Months of torture, how many such!
Weary weeks of the stick and crutch;
And still a glint in the steel blue eye
Told of a spirit that wouldn't die.

And didn't. Nay, more! in death's despite
The crippled skeleton learned to write.
"Dear Mother," at first of course; and then
"Dear Captain," inquiring about "the men."
Captain's answer: "Of eighty and five,
Giffen and I are left alive."

Word of gloom from the war one day:
"Johnston's pressed at the front, they say!"
Little Giffen was up and away;
A tear—his first—as he bade good-bye,
Dimmed the glint of his steel blue eye.
"I'll write, if spared!" There was news of the fight;
But none of Giffen—he did not write.

I sometimes fancy that, were I king
Of the princely knights of the Golden Ring,
With the song of the minstrel in mine ear,
And the tender legend that trembles here,
I'd give the best, on his bended knee,
The whitest soul of my chivalry,
For Little Giffen of Tennessee.

A Battle Ballad
To General J. E. Johnston

A summer Sunday morning,
   July the twenty-first,
In eighteen hundred sixty-one,
   The storm of battle burst.

For many a year the thunder
   Had muttered deep and low,
And many a year, through hope and fear,
   The storm had gathered slow.

Now hope had fled the hopeful,
   And fear was with the past;
And on Manassas' cornfields
   The tempest broke at last.

A wreath above the pine tops,
   The booming of a gun;
A ripple on the cornfields,
   And the battle was begun.

A feint upon our center,
   While the foeman massed his might,
For our swift and sure destruction,
   With his overwhelming "right."

All the summer air was darkened
   With the tramping of their host:

All the Sunday stillness broken
　By the clamor of their boast.
With their lips of savage shouting,
　And their eyes of sullen wrath,
Goliath, with the weaver-beam,
　The champion of Gath.

Are they men who guard the passes,
　On our "left" so far away?
In the cornfields, O Manassas!
　Are they *men* who fought today?

Our *boys* are brave and gentle,
　And their brows are smooth and white;
Have they grown to *men*, Manassas,
　In the watches of a night?

Beyond the grassy hillocks
　There are tents that glimmer white;
Beneath the leafy covert
　There is steel that glistens bright.

There are eyes of watchful reapers
　Beneath the summer leaves,
With a glitter as of sickles
　Impatient for the sheaves.

They are men who guard the passes,
　They are men who bar the ford;
Stands our David at Manassas,
　The champion of the Lord.

They are men who guard our altars,
　And beware, ye sons of Gath,
The deep and dreadful silence
　Of the lion in your path.

Lo! the foe was mad for slaughter,
　And the whirlwind hurtled on;

But our *boys* had grown to heroes,
 They were *lions*, every one.

And they stood a wall of iron,
 And they shone a wall of flame,
And they beat the baffled tempest
 To the caverns whence it came.

And Manassas' sun descended
 On their armies crushed and torn,
On a battle bravely ended,
 On a nation grandly born.

The laurel and the cypress,
 The glory and the grave,
We pledge to thee, O Liberty!
 The life blood of the brave.

The Virginians of the Valley

The knightliest of the knightly race
 That, since the days of old,
Have kept the lamp of chivalry
 Alight in hearts of gold;
The kindliest of the kindly band
 That, rarely hating ease,
Yet rode with Spotswood round the land,
 And Raleigh round the seas;

Who climbed the blue Virginian hills
 Against embattled foes,
And planted there, in valleys fair,
 The lily and the rose;
Whose fragrance lives in many lands,
 Whose beauty stars the earth,
And lights the hearths of happy homes
 With loveliness and worth.

We thought they slept! — the sons who kept
 The names of noble sires,

And slumbered while the darkness crept
　　Around their vigil fires;
But aye the "Golden Horseshoe" knights
　　Their old Dominion keep,
Whose foes have found enchanted ground,
　　But not a knight asleep!

"Our Left"

From dawn to dark they stood
　　That long midsummer day,
　　　　While fierce and fast
　　　　The battle blast
　　Swept rank on rank away.

From dawn to dark they fought,
　　With legions torn and cleft;
　　　　And still the wide
　　　　Black battle tide
　　Poured deadlier on "Our Left."

They closed each ghastly gap;
　　They dressed each shattered rank;
　　　　They knew—how well—
　　　　That freedom fell
　　With that exhausted flank.

"Oh, for a thousand men
　　Like these that melt away!"
　　　　And down they came,
　　　　With steel and flame,
　　Four thousand to the fray!

Right through the blackest cloud
　　Their lightning path they cleft;
　　　　And triumph came
　　　　With deathless fame
　　To our unconquered "Left."

Ye of your sons secure,
    Ye of your dead bereft—
    Honor the brave
    Who died to save
Your all upon "Our Left."

HERMAN MELVILLE (1819–1891). Author of *Moby-Dick*. Melville's poetry has gained growing recognition in recent years. All his Civil War poems are from *Battle-Pieces and Aspects of the War,* published in 1866.

The Portent

Hanging from the beam,
    Slowly swaying (such the law),
Gaunt the shadow on your green,
    Shenandoah!
The cut is on the crown
(Lo, John Brown),
And the stabs shall heal no more.

Hidden in the cap
    Is the anguish none can draw;
So your future veils its face,
    Shenandoah!
But the streaming beard is shown
(Weird John Brown),
The meteor of the war.

The March into Virginia

Ending in the First Manassas

Did all the lets and bars appear
    To every just or larger end,
Whence should come the trust and cheer?
    Youth must its ignorant impulse lend—
Age finds place in the rear.
    All wars are boyish, and are fought by boys,

The champions and enthusiasts of the state:
  Turbid ardors and vain joys
    Not barrenly abate—
  Stimulants to the power mature,
    Preparatives of fate.

Who here forecasteth the event?
What heart but spurns at precedent
And warnings of the wise,
Contemned foreclosures of surprise?

The banners play, the bugles call,
The air is blue and prodigal.
  No berrying party, pleasure-wooed,
No picnic party in the May,
Ever went less loth than they
  Into that leafy neighborhood.
In Bacchic glee they file toward Fate,
Moloch's uninitiate;
Expectancy, and glad surmise
Of battle's unknown mysteries.
All they feel is this: 'tis glory,
A rapture sharp, though transitory,
Yet lasting in belaureled story.
So they gayly go to fight,
Chatting left and laughing right.

But some who this blithe mood present,
  As on in lightsome files they fare,
Shall die experienced ere three days are spent—
  Perish, enlightened by the vollied glare;
Or shame survive, and, like to adamant,
  The throe of Second Manassas share.

Ball's Bluff

A Reverie

One noonday, at my window in the town,
  I saw a sight—saddest that eyes can see—

Young soldiers marching lustily
                    Unto the wars,
With fifes, and flags in mottoed pageantry;
        While all the porches, walks, and doors
Were rich with ladies cheering royally.

They moved like Juny morning on the wave,
    Their hearts were fresh as clover in its prime
    (It was the breezy summer time),
                Life throbbed so strong,
How should they dream that Death in a rosy clime
        Would come to thin their shining throng?
Youth feels immortal, like the gods sublime.

Weeks passed; and at my window, leaving bed,
    By night I mused, of easeful sleep bereft,
    On those brave boys (Ah War! thy theft);
                Some marching feet
Found pause at last by cliffs Potomac cleft;
        Wakeful I mused, while in the street
Far footfalls died away till none were left.

Shiloh

A Requiem

Skimming lightly, wheeling still,
    The swallows fly low
Over the field in clouded days,
    The forest-field of Shiloh—
Over the field where April rain
Solaced the parched ones stretched in pain
Through the pause of night
That followed the Sunday fight
    Around the church of Shiloh—
The church so lone, the log-built one,
That echoed to many a parting groan
        And natural prayer
    Of dying foemen mingled there—

Foemen at morn, but friends at eve—
    Fame or country least their care:
(What like a bullet can undeceive!)
    But now they lie low,
While over them the swallows skim,
    And all is hushed at Shiloh.

Malvern Hill

Ye elms that wave on Malvern Hill
    In prime of morn and May,
Recall ye how McClellan's men
    Here stood at bay?
While deep within yon forest dim
    Our rigid comrades lay—
Some with the cartridge in their mouth,
Others with fixed arms lifted South—
    Invoking so
The cypress glades? Ah wilds of woe!

The spires of Richmond, late beheld
    Through rifts in musket-haze,
Were closed from view in clouds of dust
    On leaf-walled ways,
Where streamed our wagons in caravan;
    And the Seven Nights and Days
Of march and fast, retreat and fight,
Pinched our grimed faces to ghastly plight—
    Does the elm wood
Recall the haggard beards of blood?

The battle-smoked flag, with stars eclipsed,
    We followed (it never fell!)—
In silence husbanded our strength—
    Received their yell;
Till on this slope we patient turned
    With cannon ordered well;

Reverse we proved was not defeat;
But ah, the sod what thousands meet! —
  Does Malvern Wood
Bethink itself, and muse and brood?

> *We elms of Malvern Hill*
>   *Remember everything;*
> *But sap the twig will fill;*
> *Wag the world how it will,*
>   *Leaves must be green in Spring.*

Stonewall Jackson

Mortally wounded at Chancellorsville

The Man who fiercest charged in fight,
  Whose sword and prayer were long —
        Stonewall!
  Even him who stoutly stood for Wrong,
How can we praise? Yet coming days
  Shall not forget him with this song.

Dead is the Man whose Cause is dead,
  Vainly he died and set his seal —
        Stonewall!
  Earnest in error, as we feel;
True to the thing he deemed was due,
  True as John Brown or steel.

Relentlessly he routed us;
  But *we* relent, for he is low —
        Stonewall!
  Justly his fame we outlaw; so
We drop a tear on the bold Virginian's bier,
  Because no wreath we owe.

A Dirge for McPherson

Killed in front of Atlanta

Arms reversed and banners craped—
    Muffled drums;
Snowy horses sable-draped—
    McPherson comes.
        But, tell us, shall we know him more,
        Lost-Mountain and lone Kenesaw?

Brave the sword upon the pall—
    A gleam in gloom;
So a bright name lighteth all
    McPherson's doom.

Bear him through the chapel door—
    Let priest in stole
Pace before the warrior
    Who led. Bell—toll!

Lay him down within the nave,
    The Lesson read—
Man is noble, man is brave,
    But man 's—a weed.

Take him up again and wend
    Graveward, nor weep:
There's a trumpet that shall rend
    This Soldier's sleep.

Pass the ropes the coffin round,
    And let descend;
Prayer and volley—let it sound
    McPherson's end.
        True fame is his, for life is o'er—
        Sarpedon of the mighty war.

Sheridan at Cedar Creek

Shoe the steed with silver
  That bore him to the fray,
When he heard the guns at dawning—
  Miles away;
When he heard them calling, calling—
  Mount! nor stay:
      Quick, or all is lost;
      They've surprised and stormed the post,
      They push your routed host—
Gallop! retrieve the day.

House the horse in ermine—
  For the foam-flake blew
White through the red October;
  He thundered into view;
They cheered him in the looming,
  Horseman and horse they knew.
      The turn of the tide began,
      The rally of bugles ran,
      He swung his hat in the van;
The electric hoof-spark flew.

Wreathe the steed and lead him—
  For the charge he led
Touched and turned the cypress
  Into amaranths for the head
Of Philip, king of riders,
  Who raised them from the dead.
      The camp (at dawning lost)
      By eve, recovered—forced,
      Rang with laughter of the host
As belated Early fled.

Shroud the horse in sable—
  For the mounds they heap!
There is firing in the Valley,
  And yet no strife they keep;

It is the parting volley,
　It is the pathos deep.
　　There is glory for the brave
　　Who lead, and nobly save,
　　But no knowledge in the grave
Where the nameless followers sleep.

"Formerly a Slave"

An idealized Portrait, by E. Vedder, in the Spring Exhibition
of the National Academy, 1865

　The sufferance of her race is shown,
　　And retrospect of life,
　Which now too late deliverance dawns upon;
　　Yet is she not at strife.

　Her children's children they shall know
　　The good withheld from her;
　And so her reverie takes prophetic cheer—
　　In spirit she sees the stir

　Far down the depth of thousand years,
　　And marks the revel shine;
　Her dusky face is lit with sober light,
　　Sibylline, yet benign.

Rebel Color-bearers at Shiloh

A plea against the vindictive cry raised by civilians shortly
after the surrender at Appomattox

　The color-bearers facing death
　White in the whirling sulphurous wreath,
　　Stand boldly out before the line;
　Right and left their glances go,
　Proud of each other, glorying in their show;

Their battle-flags about them blow,
   And fold them as in flame divine:
Such living robes are only seen
Round martyrs burning on the green—
And martyrs for the Wrong have been.

Perish their Cause! but mark the men—
Mark the planted statues, then
Draw trigger on them if you can.

The leader of a patriot-band
Even so could view rebels who so could stand;
   And this when peril pressed him sore,
Left aidless in the shivered front of war—
  Skulkers behind, defiant foes before,
And fighting with a broken brand.
The challenge in that courage rare—
Courage defenseless, proudly bare—
Never could tempt him; he could dare
Strike up the leveled rifle there.

Sunday at Shiloh, and the day
When Stonewall charged—McClellan's crimson May,
And Chickamauga's wave of death,
And of the Wilderness the cypress wreath—
     All these have passed away.
The life in the veins of Treason lags,
Her daring color-bearers drop their flags,
  And yield. *Now* shall we fire?
     Can poor spite be?
Shall nobleness in victory less aspire
Than in reverse? Spare Spleen her ire,
    And think how Grant met Lee.

On the Slain at Chickamauga

Happy are they and charmed in life
   Who through long wars arrive unscarred

At peace. To such the wreath be given,
If they unfalteringly have striven —
   In honor, as in limb, unmarred.
Let cheerful praise be rife,
   And let them live their years at ease,
Musing on brothers who victorious died —
   Loved mates whose memory shall ever please.

And yet mischance is honorable too —
   Seeming defeat in conflict justified
Whose end to closing eyes is hid from view.
The will, that never can relent —
The aim, survivor of the bafflement,
      Make this memorial due.

The Surrender at Appomattox

As billows upon billows roll,
   On victory victory breaks;
Ere yet seven days from Richmond's fall
   And crowning triumph wakes
The loud joy-gun, whose thunders run
   By sea shore, streams, and lakes.
      The hope and great event agree
      In the sword that Grant received from Lee.

The warring eagles fold the wing,
   But not in Cæsar's sway;
Not Rome o'ercome by Roman arms we sing,
   As on Pharsalia's day,
But Treason thrown, though a giant grown,
   And Freedom's larger play.
      All human tribes glad token see
      In the close of the wars of Grant and Lee.

JAMES JEFFREY ROCHE (1847–1908). Poet and journalist. Roche was a popular contributor to such leading periodicals as the *Atlantic Monthly* and *Harper's*.

Gettysburg

There was no union in the land,
    Though wise men labored long
With links of clay and ropes of sand
    To bind the right and wrong.

There was no temper in the blade
    That once could cleave a chain;
Its edge was dull with touch of trade
    And clogged with rust of gain.

The sand and clay must shrink away
    Before the lava tide:
By blows and blood and fire assay
    The metal must be tried.

Here sledge and anvil met, and when
    The furnace fiercest roared,
God's undiscerning workingmen
    Reforged His people's sword.

Enough for them to ask and know
    The moment's duty clear—
The bayonets flashed it there below,
    The guns proclaimed it here:

To do and dare, and die at need,
    But while life lasts, to fight—
For right or wrong a simple creed,
    But simplest for the right.

They faltered not who stood that day
    And held this post of dread;
Nor cowards they who wore the gray
    Until the gray was red.

For every wreath the victor wears
    The vanquished half may claim;

And every monument declares
　A common pride and fame.

We raise no altar stones to Hate,
　Who never bowed to Fear:
No province crouches at our gate,
　To shame our triumph here.

Here standing by a dead wrong's grave
　The blindest now may see,
The blow that liberates the slave
　But sets the master free!

When ills beset the nation's life
　Too dangerous to bear,
The sword must be the surgeon's knife,
　Too merciful to spare.

O Soldier of our common land,
　'T is thine to bear that blade
Loose in the sheath, or firm in hand,
　But ever unafraid.

When foreign foes assail our right,
　One nation trusts to thee—
To wield it well in worthy fight—
　The sword of Meade and Lee!

WILL HENRY THOMPSON (1848–1918). Thompson's famous poem commemorates Pickett's courageous though doomed charge on the Union center at Gettysburg, the decisive moment in the battle and a turning point in the war.

The High Tide at Gettysburg

A cloud possessed the hollow field,
The gathering battle's smoky shield:
　Athwart the gloom the lightning flashed,
　And through the cloud some horsemen dashed,
And from the heights the thunder pealed.

Then, at the brief command of Lee,
Moved out that matchless infantry,
  With Pickett leading grandly down,
  To rush against the roaring crown
Of those dread heights of destiny.

Far heard above the angry guns,
A cry of tumult runs:
  The voice that rang through Shiloh's woods,
  And Chickamauga's solitudes:
The fierce South cheering on her sons!

Ah, how the withering tempest blew
Against the front of Pettigrew!
  A Khamsin wind that scorched and singed,
  Like that infernal flame that fringed
The British squares at Waterloo!

A thousand fell where Kemper led;
A thousand died where Garnett bled;
  In blinding flame and strangling smoke,
  The remnant through the batteries broke,
And crossed the works with Armistead.

"Once more in Glory's van with me!"
Virginia cried to Tennessee:
  "We two together, come what may,
  Shall stand upon those works today!"
The reddest day in history.

Brave Tennessee! In reckless way
Virginia heard her comrade say:
  "Close round this rent and riddled rag!"
  What time she set her battle flag
Amid the guns of Doubleday.

But who shall break the guards that wait
Before the awful face of Fate?
  The tattered standards of the South
  Were shrivelled at the cannon's mouth,
And all her hopes were desolate.

In vain the Tennesseean set
His breast against the bayonet;
    In vain Virginia charged and raged,
    A tigress in her wrath uncaged,
Till all the hill was red and wet!

Above the bayonets, mixed and crossed,
Men saw a gray, gigantic ghost
    Receding through the battle-cloud,
    And heard across the tempest loud
The death-cry of a nation lost!

The brave went down! Without disgrace
They leaped to Ruin's red embrace;
    They only heard Fame's thunders wake,
    And saw the dazzling sunburst break
In smiles on Glory's bloody face!

They fell, who lifted up a hand
And bade the sun in heaven to stand;
    They smote and fell, who set the bars
    Against the progress of the stars,
And stayed the march of Motherland.

They stood, who saw the future come
On through the fight's delirium;
    They smote and stood, who held the hope
    Of nations on that slippery slope,
Amid the cheers of Christendom!

God lives! He forged the iron will,
    That clutched and held that trembling hill!
    God lives and reigns! He built and lent
    The heights for Freedom's battlement,
Where floats her flag in triumph still!

Fold up the banners! Smelt the guns!
Love rules. Her gentler purpose runs.
    A mighty mother turns in tears,
    The pages of her battle years,
Lamenting all her fallen sons!

LLOYD MIFFLIN (1846–1921). Mifflin was known particularly for his sonnets. Gettysburg is the subject of his sonnet, "The Battlefield."

The Battlefield

Those were the conquered, still too proud to yield—
These were the victors, yet too poor for shrouds!
Here scarlet Slaughter slew her countless crowds
Heaped high in ranks where'er the hot guns pealed.
The brooks that wandered through the battlefield
Flowed slowly on in ever-reddening streams;
Here where the rank wheat waves and golden gleams,
The dreadful squadrons, thundering, charged and reeled.
Within the blossoming clover many a bone
Lying unsepulchred, has bleached to white;
While gentlest hearts that only love had known,
Have ached with anguish at the awful sight;
And War's gaunt Vultures that were lean, have grown
Gorged in the darkness in a single night!

EDMUND CLARENCE STEDMAN (1833–1908). Poet and critic. From 1861 to 1863, he was Washington correspondent for the New York *World*. "Kearny at Seven Pines" celebrates the heroic actions of Union officer "Phil" Kearny, who rallied the Union troops to victory at Fair Oaks in May 1862.

Sumter

Came the morning of that day
When the God to whom we pray
Gave the soul of Henry Clay
        To the land;
How we loved him, living, dying!
But his birthday banners flying
Saw us asking and replying
        Hand to hand.

For we knew that far away,
Round the fort in Charleston Bay,
Hung the dark impending fray,
        Soon to fall;

And that Sumter's brave defender
Had the summons to surrender
Seventy loyal hearts and tender—
    (Those were all!)

And we knew the April sun
Lit the length of many a gun—
Hosts of batteries to the one
    Island crag;
Guns and mortars grimly frowning,
Johnson, Moultrie, Pinckney, crowning,
And ten thousand men disowning
    The old flag.

Oh, the fury of the fight
Even then was at its height!
Yet no breath, from noon till night,
    Reached us here;
We had almost ceased to wonder,
And the day had faded under,
When the echo of the thunder
    Filled each ear!

Then our hearts more fiercely beat,
As we crowded on the street,
Hot to gather and repeat
    All the tale;
All the doubtful chances turning,
Till our souls with shame were burning,
As if twice our bitter yearning
    Could avail!

Who had fired the earliest gun?
Was the fort by traitors won?
Was there succor? What was done?
    Who could know?
And once more our thoughts would wander
To the gallant, lone commander,
On his battered ramparts grander
    Than the foe.

Not too long the brave shall wait:
On their own heads be their fate,
Who against the hallowed State
    Dare begin;
Flag defied and compact riven!
In the record of high Heaven
How shall Southern men be shriven
    For the sin!

Kearny at Seven Pines

So that soldierly legend is still on its journey—
    That story of Kearny who knew not to yield!
'T was the day when with Jameson, fierce Berry, and Birney,
    Against twenty thousand he rallied the field.
Where the red volleys poured, where the clamor rose highest,
    Where the dead lay in clumps through the dwarf oak and pine,
Where the aim from the thicket was surest and nighest—
    No charge like Phil Kearny's along the whole line.

When the battle went ill, and the bravest were solemn,
    Near the dark Seven Pines, where we still held our ground,
He rode down the length of the withering column,
    And his heart at our war-cry leapt up with a bound;
He snuffed, like his charger, the wind of the powder—
    His sword waved us on and we answered the sign;
Loud our cheer as we rushed, but his laugh rang the louder.
    "There's the devil's own fun, boys, along the whole line!"

How he strode his brown steed! How we saw his blade brighten,
    In the one hand still left—and the reins in his teeth!
He laughed like a boy when the holidays heighten,
    But a soldier's glance shot from his visor beneath.
Up came the reserves to the mellay infernal,
    Asking where to go in—through the clearing or pine?
"Oh, anywhere! Forward! 'T is all the same, Colonel:
    You'll find lovely fighting along the whole line!"

Oh, evil the black shroud of night at Chantilly,
    That hid him from sight of his brave men and tried!

Foul, foul sped the bullet that clipped the white lily,
    The flower of our knighthood, the whole army's pride!
Yet we dream that he still—in that shadowy region
    Where the dead form their ranks at the wan drummer's sign—
Rides on, as of old, down the length of his legion,
    And the word still is "Forward!" along the whole line.

MADISON CAWEIN (1865–1914). Cawein's rousing poem commemorates the daring raid (one of many) on the Union lines in March 1863 by the legendary Captain John S. Mosby and his guerrilla fighters.

Mosby at Hamilton

Down Loudon Lanes, with swinging reins
    And clash of spur and sabre,
And bugling of the battle horn,
Six score and eight we rode at morn,
Six score and eight of Southern born,
    All tried in love and labor.

Full in the sun at Hamilton,
    We met the South's invaders;
Who, over fifteen hundred strong,
'Mid blazing homes had marched along
All night, with Northern shout and song
    To crush the rebel raiders.

Down Loudon Lanes, with streaming manes,
    We spurred in wild March weather;
And all along our war-scarred way
The graves of Southern heroes lay,
Our guide-posts to revenge that day,
    As we rode grim together.

Old tales still tell some miracle
    Of saints in holy writing—
But who shall say while hundreds fled
Before the few that Mosby led,
Unless the noblest of our dead
    Charged with us then when fighting?

While Yankee cheers still stunned our ears,
    Of troops at Harper's Ferry,
While Sheridan led on his Huns,
And Richmond rocked to roaring guns,
We felt the South still had some sons
    She would not scorn to bury.

JOHN REUBEN THOMPSON (1823–1873). Poet, editor, and journalist.
Thompson owned the *Southern Literary Messenger* and published works by the
South's leading writers.

Lee to the Rear

Dawn of a pleasant morning in May
Broke through the Wilderness cool and gray;
While perched in the tallest tree-tops, the birds
Were carolling Mendelssohn's "Song without Words."

Far from the haunts of men remote,
The brook brawled on with a liquid note;
And Nature, all tranquil and lovely, wore
The smile of the spring, as in Eden of yore.

Little by little, as daylight increased,
And deepened the roseate flush in the East—
Little by little did morning reveal
Two long glittering lines of steel;

Where two hundred thousand bayonets gleam,
Tipped with the light of the earliest beam,
And the faces are sullen and grim to see
In the hostile armies of Grant and Lee.

All of a sudden, ere rose the sun,
Pealed on the silence the opening gun—
A little white puff of smoke there came,
And anon the valley was wreathed in flame.

Down on the left of the Rebel lines,
Where a breastwork stands in a copse of pines,

Before the Rebels their ranks can form,
The Yankees have carried the place by storm.

Stars and Stripes on the salient wave,
Where many a hero has found a grave,
And the gallant Confederates strive in vain
The ground they have drenched with their blood, to regain.

Yet louder the thunder of battle roared—
Yet a deadlier fire on the columns poured;
Slaughter infernal rode with Despair,
Furies twain, through the murky air.

Not far off, in the saddle there sat
A gray-bearded man in a black slouched hat;
Not much moved by the fire was he,
Calm and resolute Robert Lee.

Quick and watchful he kept his eye
On the bold Rebel brigades close by—
Reserves that were standing (and dying) at ease,
While the tempest of wrath toppled over the trees.

For still with their loud, deep, bull-dog bay,
The Yankee batteries blazed away,
And with every murderous second that sped
A dozen brave fellows, alas! fell dead.

The grand old graybeard rode to the space
Where Death and his victims stood face to face,
And silently waved his old slouched hat—
A world of meaning there was in that!

"Follow me! Steady! We'll save the day!"
This was what he seemed to say;
And to the light of his glorious eye
The bold brigades thus made reply:

"We'll go forward, but you must go back"—
And they moved not an inch in the perilous track:
"Go to the rear, and we'll send them to hell!"
And the sound of the battle was lost in their yell.

Turning his bridle, Robert Lee
Rode to the rear. Like waves of the sea,
Bursting the dikes in their overflow,
Madly his veterans dashed on the foe.

And backward in terror that foe was driven,
Their banners rent and their columns riven,
Wherever the tide of battle rolled
Over the Wilderness, wood and wold.

Sunset out of a crimson sky
Streamed o'er a field of ruddier dye,
And the brook ran on with a purple stain,
From the blood of ten thousand foemen slain.

Seasons have passed since that day and year—
Again o'er its pebbles the brook runs clear,
And the field in a richer green is drest
Where the dead of a terrible conflict rest.

Hushed is the roll of the Rebel drum,
The sabres are sheathed, and the cannon are dumb;
And Fate, with his pitiless hand, has furled
The flag that once challenged the gaze of the world;

But the fame of the Wilderness fight abides;
And down into history grandly rides,
Calm and unmoved as in battle he sat,
The gray-bearded man in the black slouched hat.

HENRY WADSWORTH LONGFELLOW (1807–1882). The most popular American poet of his time, author of "The Song of Hiawatha" and "Evangeline." "The Cumberland" recounts the sinking of the 24-gun Union sloop by the *Merrimac* in March 1862.

Killed at the Ford

He is dead, the beautiful youth,
The heart of honor, the tongue of truth,
He, the life and light of us all,

Whose voice was blithe as a bugle-call,
Whom all eyes followed with one consent,
The cheer of whose laugh, and whose pleasant word,
Hushed all murmurs of discontent.

Only last night, as we rode along,
Down the dark of the mountain gap,
To visit the picket-guard at the ford,
Little dreaming of any mishap,
He was humming the words of some old song:
"Two red roses he had on his cap
And another he bore at the point of his sword."

Sudden and swift a whistling ball
Came out of a wood, and the voice was still;
Something I heard in the darkness fall,
And for a moment my blood grew chill;
I spake in a whisper, as he who speaks
In a room where some one is lying dead;
But he made no answer to what I said.

We lifted him up to his saddle again,
And through the mire and the mist and the rain
Carried him back to the silent camp,
And laid him as if asleep on his bed;
And I saw by the light of the surgeon's lamp
Two white roses upon his cheeks,
And one, just over his heart, blood red!

And I saw in a vision how far and fleet
That fatal bullet went speeding forth,
Till it reached a town in the distant North,
Till it reached a house in a sunny street,
Till it reached a heart that ceased to beat
Without a murmur, without a cry;
And a bell was tolled, in that far-off town,
For one who had passed from cross to crown,
And the neighbors wondered that she should die.

The Cumberland

At anchor in Hampton Roads we lay,
　　On board of the Cumberland, sloop-of-war;
And at times from the fortress across the bay
　　　The alarum of drums swept past,
　　　Or a bugle blast
　　From the camp on the shore.

Then far away to the south uprose
　　A little feather of snow-white smoke,
And we knew that the iron ship of our foes
　　　Was steadily steering its course
　　　To try the force
　　Of our ribs of oak.

Down upon us heavily runs,
　　Silent and sullen, the floating fort;
Then comes a puff of smoke from her guns,
　　　And leaps the terrible death,
　　　With fiery breath,
　　From each open port.

We are not idle, but send her straight
　　Defiance back in a full broadside!
As hail rebounds from a roof of slate,
　　　Rebounds our heavier hail
　　　From each iron scale
　　Of the monster's hide.

"Strike your flag!" the rebel cries
　　In his arrogant old plantation strain.
"Never!" our gallant Morris replies:
　　　"It is better to sink than to yield!"
　　　And the whole air pealed
　　With the cheers of our men.

Then, like a kraken huge and black,
　　She crushed our ribs in her iron grasp!
Down went the Cumberland all awrack,

With a sudden shudder of death,
And the cannon's breath
For her dying gasp.

Next morn, as the sun rose over the bay,
Still floated our flag at the mainmast head.
Lord, how beautiful was Thy day!
Every waft of the air
Was a whisper of prayer,
Or a dirge for the dead.

Ho! brave hearts that went down in the seas!
Ye are at peace in the troubled stream;
Ho! brave land! with hearts like theses,
Thy flag, that is rent in twain,
Shall be one again,
And without a seam!

HENRY HOWARD BROWNELL (1820–1872). Poet and historian. "The Bay Fight," one of the most famous battle poems of the war, recounts in detail the battle of Mobile Bay in August 1864.

The Bay Fight

Three days through sapphire seas we sailed,
The steady Trade blew strong and free,
The Northern Light his banners paled,
The Ocean Stream our channels wet,
We rounded low Canaveral's lee,
And passed the isles of emerald set
In blue Bahama's turquoise sea.

By reef and shoal obscurely mapped,
The hauntings of the gray sea-wolf,
The palmy Western Key lay lapped
In the warm washing of the Gulf.

But weary to the hearts of all
The burning glare, the barren reach

Of Santa Rosa's withered beach,
And Pensacola's ruined wall.

And weary was the long patrol,
　　The thousand miles of shapeless strand,
From Brazos to San Blas that roll
　　Their drifting dunes of desert sand.

Yet coastwise as we cruised or lay,
　　The land-breeze still at nightfall bore,
By beach and fortress-guarded bay,
　　Sweet odors from the enemy's shore,

Fresh from the forest solitudes,
　　Unchallenged of his sentry lines—
The bursting of his cypress buds,
　　And the warm fragrance of his pines.

Ah, never braver bark and crew,
　　Nor bolder Flag a foe to dare,
Had left a wake on ocean blue
　　Since Lion-Heart sailed Trenc-le-mer!

But little gain by that dark ground
　　Was ours, save, sometimes, freer breath
For friend or brother strangely found,
　　'Scaped from the drear domain of death.

And little venture for the bold,
　　Or laurel for our valiant Chief,
　　Save some blockaded British thief,
Full fraught with murder in his hold,

Caught unawares at ebb or flood,
　　Or dull bombardment, day by day,
　　With fort and earthwork, far away,
Low couched in sullen leagues of mud.

A weary time—but to the strong
　　The day at last, as ever, came;
And the volcano, laid so long,
　　Leaped forth in thunder and in flame!

"*Man your starboard battery!*"
Kimberly shouted;
The ship, with her hearts of oak,
Was going, 'mid roar and smoke,
On to victory;
None of us doubted,
No, not our dying—
Farragut's Flag was flying!

Gaines growled low on our left,
Morgan roared on our right;
Before us, gloomy and fell,
With breath like the fume of hell,
Lay the dragon of iron shell,
Driven at last to the fight!

Ha, old ship! do they thrill,
The brave two hundred scars
You got in the River-Wars?
That were leeched with clamorous skill
(Surgery savage and hard),
Splinted with bolt and beam,
Probed in scarfing and seam,
Rudely linted and tarred
With oakum and boiling pitch,
And sutured with splice and hitch,
At the Brooklyn Navy Yard!

Our lofty spars were down,
To bide the battle's frown
(Wont of old renown)—
But every ship was drest
In her bravest and her best,
As if for a July day;
Sixty flags and three,
As we floated up the bay—
At every peak and mast-head flew
The brave Red, White, and Blue—
We were eighteen ships that day.

With hawsers strong and taut,
The weaker lashed to port,

On we sailed two by two—
That if either a bolt should feel
Crash through caldron or wheel,
Fin of bronze, or sinew of steel,
Her mate might bear her through.

Forging boldly ahead,
The great Flag-Ship led,
Grandest of sights!
On her lofty mizzen flew
Our leader's dauntless Blue,
That had waved o'er twenty fights.
So we went with the first of the tide,
Slowly, 'mid the roar
Of the rebel guns ashore
And the thunder of each full broadside.

Ah, how poor the prate
Of statute and state
We once held these fellows!
Here on the flood's pale green,
Hark how he bellows,
Each bluff old Sea-Lawyer!
Talk to them, Dahlgren,
Parrott, and Sawyer!

On, in the whirling shade
Of the cannon's sulphury breath,
We drew to the Line of Death
That our devilish Foe had laid—
Meshed in a horrible net,
And baited villainous well,
Right in our path were set
Three hundred traps of hell!

And there, O sight forlorn!
There, while the cannon
Hurtled and thundered
(Ah, what ill raven
Flapped o'er the ship that morn!)—
Caught by the under-death,

In the drawing of a breath
Down went dauntless Craven,
He and his hundred!

A moment we saw her turret,
A little heel she gave,
And a thin white spray went o'er her,
Like the crest of a breaking wave;
In that great iron coffin,
The channel for their grave,
The fort their monument
(Seen afar in the offing),
Ten fathom deep lie Craven
And the bravest of our brave.

Then in that deadly track
A little the ships held back,
Closing up in their stations;
There are minutes that fix the fate
Of battles and of nations
(Christening the generations),
When valor were all too late,
If a moment's doubt be harbored;
From the main-top, bold and brief,
Came the word of our grand old chief:
"Go on!"—'t was all he said—
Our helm was put to starboard,
And the Hartford passed ahead.

Ahead lay the Tennessee,
On our starboard bow he lay,
With his mail-clad consorts three
(The rest had run up the bay);
There he was, belching flame from his bow,
And the steam from his throat's abyss
Was a Dragon's maddened hiss;
In sooth a most cursed craft!—
In a sullen ring, at bay,
By the Middle-Ground they lay,
Raking us fore and aft.
Trust me, our berth was hot,

Ah, wickedly well they shot—
How their death-bolts howled and stung!
And the water-batteries played
With their deadly cannonade
Till the air around us rung;
So the battle raged and roared;
Ah, had you been aboard
To have seen the fight we made!
How they leapt, the tongues of flame,
From the cannon's fiery lip!
How the broadsides, deck and frame,
Shook the great ship!

And how the enemy's shell
Came crashing, heavy and oft,
Clouds of splinters flying aloft
And falling in oaken showers;
But ah, the pluck of the crew!
Had you stood on that deck of ours
You had seen what men may do.

Still, as the fray grew louder,
Boldly they worked and well—
Steadily came the powder,
Steadily came the shell.
And if tackle or truck found hurt,
Quickly they cleared the wreck—
And the dead were laid to port,
All a-row, on our deck.

Never a nerve that failed,
Never a cheek that paled,
Not a tinge of gloom or pallor;
There was bold Kentucky's grit,
And the old Virginian valor,
And the daring Yankee wit.
There were blue eyes from turfy Shannon,
  There were black orbs from palmy Niger—
  But there alongside the cannon,
    Each man fought like a tiger!
    A little, once, it looked ill,

Our consort began to burn—
They quenched the flames with a will,
But our men were falling still,
And still the fleet were astern.

Right abreast of the Fort
In an awful shroud they lay,
Broadsides thundering away,
And lightning from every port;
Scene of glory and dread!
A storm-cloud all aglow
With flashes of fiery red,
The thunder raging below,
And the forest of flags o'erhead!

So grand the hurly and roar,
So fiercely their broadsides blazed,
The regiments fighting ashore
Forgot to fire as they gazed.

There, to silence the foe,
Moving grimly and slow,
They loomed in that deadly wreath,
Where the darkest batteries frowned—
Death in the air all round,
And the black torpedoes beneath!

And now, as we looked ahead,
All for'ard, the long white deck
Was growing a strange dull red—
But soon, as once and again
Fore and aft we sped
(The firing to guide or check),
You could hardly choose but tread
On the ghastly human wreck
(Dreadful gobbet and shred
That a minute ago were men!),
Red, from mainmast to bitts!
Red, on bulwark and wale,
Red, by combing and hatch,
Red, o'er netting and vail!

And ever, with steady con,
The ship forged slowly by—
And ever the crew fought on,
And their cheers rang loud and high.

Grand was the sight to see
How by their guns they stood,
Right in front of our dead,
Fighting square abreast—
Each brawny arm and chest
All spotted with black and red,
Chrism of fire and blood!

Worth our watch, dull and sterile,
Worth all the weary time,
Worth the woe and the peril,
To stand in that strait sublime!

Fear? A forgotten form!
Death? A dream of the eyes!
We were atoms in God's great storm
That roared through the angry skies.

One only doubt was ours,
One only dread we knew—
Could the day that dawned so well
Go down for the Darker Powers?
Would the fleet get through?
And ever the shot and shell
Came with the howl of hell,
The splinter-clouds rose and fell,
And the long line of corpses grew—
Would the fleet win through?

They are men that never will fail
(How aforetime they've fought!),
But Murder may yet prevail—
They may sink as Craven sank.
Therewith one hard fierce thought,
Burning on heart and lip,

Ran like fire through the ship;
Fight her, to the last plank!
A dimmer renown might strike
If Death lay square alongside—
But the old Flag has no like,
She must fight, whatever betide;
When the War is a tale of old,
And this day's story is told,
They shall hear how the Hartford died!

But as we ranged ahead,
And the leading ships worked in,
Losing their hope to win,
The enemy turned and fled—
And one seeks a shallow reach!
And another, winged in her flight,
Our mate, brave Jouett, brings in;
And one, all torn in the fight,
Runs for a wreck on the beach,
Where her flames soon fire the night.

And the Ram, when well up the Bay,
And we looked that our stems should meet
(He had us fair for a prey),
Shifting his helm midway,
Sheered off, and ran for the fleet;
There, without skulking or sham,
He fought them gun for gun;
And ever he sought to ram,
But could finish never a one.

From the first of the iron shower
Till we sent our parting shell,
'T was just one savage hour
Of the roar and the rage of hell.

With the lessening smoke and thunder,
Our glasses around we aim—
What is that burning yonder?
Our Philippi—aground and in flame!

Below, 't was still all a-roar,
As the ships went by the shore,
But the fire of the Fort had slacked
(So fierce their volleys had been)—
And now with a mighty din,
The whole fleet came grandly in,
Though sorely battered and wracked.

So, up the Bay we ran,
The Flag to port and ahead—
And a pitying rain began
To wash the lips of our dead.

A league from the Fort we lay,
And deemed that the end must lag—
When lo! looking down the Bay,
There flaunted the Rebel Rag;
The Ram is again under way
And heading dead for the Flag!

Steering up with the stream,
Boldly his course he lay,
Though the fleet all answered his fire,
And, as he still drew nigher,
Ever on bow and beam
Our Monitors pounded away;
How the Chickasaw hammered away!

Quickly breasting the wave,
Eager the prize to win,
First of us all the brave
Monongahela went in
Under full head of steam;
Twice she struck him abeam,
Till her stem was a sorry work
(She might have run on a crag!),
The Lackawanna hit fair,
He flung her aside like cork,
And still he held for the Flag.
High in the mizzen shroud

(Lest the smoke his sight o'erwhelm),
Our Admiral's voice rang loud;
"Hard-a-starboard your helm!
Starboard, and run him down!"
Starboard it was—and so,
Like a black squall's lifting frown,
Our mighty bow bore down
On the iron beak of the Foe.

We stood on the deck together,
Men that had looked on death
In battle and stormy weather;
Yet a little we held our breath,
When, with the hush of death,
The great ships drew together.

Our Captain strode to the bow,
Drayton, courtly and wise,
Kindly cynic, and wise
(You hardly had known him now,
The flame of fight in his eyes!)—
His brave heart eager to feel
How the oak would tell on the steel!

But, as the space grew short,
A little he seemed to shun us;
Out peered a form grim and lanky,
And a voice yelled, *"Hard-a-port!*
Hard-a-port!—here's the damned Yankee
Coming right down on us!"

He sheered, but the ships ran foul
With a gnarring shudder and growl;
He gave us a deadly gun;
But as he passed in his pride
(Rasping right alongside!),
The old Flag, in thunder-tones
Poured in her port broadside,
Rattling his iron hide
And cracking his timber-bones!

Just then, at speed on the Foe,
With her bow all weathered and brown,
The great Lackawanna came down
Full tilt, for another blow;
We were forging ahead,
She reversed—but, for all our pains,
Rammed the old Hartford, instead,
Just for'ard the mizzen chains!

Ah! how the masts did buckle and bend,
And the stout hull ring and reel,
As she took us right on end!
(Vain were engine and wheel,
She was under full steam)—
With the roar of a thunder-stroke
Her two thousand tons of oak
Brought up on us, right abeam!

A wreck, as it looked, we lay
(Rib and plank-sheer gave way
To the stroke of that giant wedge!)—
Here, after all, we go—
The old ship is gone!—ah, no,
But cut to the water's edge.

Never mind then—at him again!
His flurry now can't last long;
He'll never again see land—
Try that on *him*, Marchand!
On him again, brave Strong!

Heading square at the hulk,
Full on his beam we bore;
But the spine of the huge Sea-Hog
Lay on the tide like a log,
He vomited flame no more.

By this, he had found it hot;
Half the fleet, in an angry ring,
Closed round the hideous thing,

Hammering with solid shot,
  And bearing down, bow on bow;
  He has but a minute to choose—
  Life or renown?—which now
  Will the Rebel Admiral lose?

Cruel, haughty, and cold,
  He ever was strong and bold;
  Shall he shrink from a wooden stem?
  He will think of that brave band
  He sank in the Cumberland;
  Ay, he will sink like them.

Nothing left but to fight
Boldly his last sea-fight!
Can he strike? By Heaven, 't is true!
Down comes the traitor Blue,
And up goes the captive White!

Up went the White! Ah, then
The hurrahs that once and again
Rang from three thousand men
All flushed and savage with fight!
Our dead lay cold and stark;
But our dying, down in the dark,
Answered as best they might,
Lifting their poor lost arms,
And cheering for God and Right!

Ended the mighty noise,
Thunder of forts and ships.
Down we went to the hold,
Oh, our dear dying boys!
How we pressed their poor brave lips
(Ah, so pallid and cold!)
And held their hands to the last
(Those who had hands to hold).

Still thee, O woman heart!
(So strong an hour ago);

If the idle tears must start,
'T is not in vain they flow.

They died, our children dear.
On the drear berth-deck they died—
Do not think of them here—
Even now their footsteps near
The immortal, tender sphere
(Land of love and cheer!
Home of the Crucified!).

And the glorious deed survives;
Our threescore, quiet and cold,
Lie thus, for a myriad lives
And treasure-millions untold
(Labor of poor men's lives,
Hunger of weans and wives,
Such is war-wasted gold).

Our ship and her fame today
Shall float on the storied Stream
When mast and shroud have crumbled away
And her long white deck is a dream.

One daring leap in the dark,
Three mortal hours, at the most—
And hell lies stiff and stark
On a hundred leagues of coast.

For the mighty Gulf is ours—
The bay is lost and won,
An Empire is lost and won!
Land, if thou yet hast flowers,
Twine them in one more wreath
Of tenderest white and red
(Twin buds of glory and death!),
For the brows of our brave dead,
For thy Navy's noblest son.

Joy, O Land, for thy sons,
Victors by flood and field!

The traitor walls and guns
Have nothing left but to yield
(Even now they surrender!).
And the ships shall sail once more,
And the cloud of war sweep on
To break on the cruel shore;
But Craven is gone,
He and his hundred are gone.

The flags flutter up and down
At sunrise and twilight dim,
The cannons menace and frown—
But never again for him,
Him and the hundred.

The Dahlgrens are dumb,
Dumb are the mortars;
Never more shall the drum
Beat to colors and quarters—
The great guns are silent.

O brave heart and loyal!
Let all your colors dip;
Mourn him proud ship!
From main deck to royal.
God rest our Captain,
Rest our lost hundred!

Droop, flag and pennant!
What is your pride for?
Heaven, that he died for,
Rest our Lieutenant,
Rest our brave threescore!

O Mother Land! this weary life
　　We led, we lead, is 'long of thee;
Thine the strong agony of strife,
　　And thine the lonely sea.

Thine the long decks all slaughter-spent,
　　The weary rows of cots that lie

With wrecks of strong men, marred and rent,
  'Neath Pensacola's sky.

And thine the iron caves and dens
  Wherein the flame our war-fleet drives;
The fiery vaults, whose breath is men's
  Most dear and precious lives!

Ah, ever when with storm sublime
  Dread Nature clears our murky air,
Thus in the crash of falling crime
  Some lesser guilt must share.

Full red the furnace fires must glow
  That melt the ore of mortal kind;
The mills of God are grinding slow,
  But ah, how close they grind!

Today the Dahlgren and the drum
  Are dread Apostles of His Name;
His kingdom here can only come
  By chrism of blood and flame.

Be strong: already slants the gold
  Athwart these wild and stormy skies;
From out this blackened waste, behold
  What happy homes shall rise!

But see thou well no traitor gloze,
  No striking hands with Death and Shame,
Betray the sacred blood that flows
  So freely for thy name.

And never fear a victor foe —
  Thy children's hearts are strong and high;
Nor mourn too fondly; well they know
  On deck or field to die.
Nor shalt thou want one willing breath,
  Though, ever smiling round the brave,
The blue sea bear us on to death,
  The green were one wide grave.

GEORGE HENRY BOKER (1823–1890). Poet, dramatist, and diplomat. Though strongly pro-Union, many of his poems, like "Dirge for a Soldier," lament the losses of both sides.

Dirge for a Soldier

Close his eyes; his work is done!
　What to him is friend or foeman,
Rise of moon, or set of sun,
　Hand of man, or kiss of woman?
　　　Lay him low, lay him low,
　　　In the clover or the snow!
　　　What cares he? he cannot know:
　　　　Lay him low!

As man may, he fought his fight,
　Proved his truth by his endeavor;
Let him sleep in solemn night,
　Sleep forever and forever.
　　　Lay him low, lay him low,
　　　In the clover or the snow!
　　　What cares he? he cannot know:
　　　　Lay him low!

Fold him in his country's stars,
　Roll the drum and fire the volley!
What to him are all our wars,
　What but death-bemocking folly?
　　　Lay him low, lay him low,
　　　In the clover or the snow!
　　　What cares he? he cannot know:
　　　　Lay him low!

Leave him to God's watching eye;
　Trust him to the hand that made him.
Mortal love weeps idly by:
　God alone has power to aid him.
　　　Lay him low, lay him low,
　　　In the clover or the snow!
　　　What cares he? he cannot know:
　　　　Lay him low!

FRANCIS MILES FINCH (1827–1907). Poet and jurist. His famous
poem "The Blue and the Gray" was inspired by the women of Columbus,
Mississippi, who decorated with flowers the graves of Confederate and Union
soldiers alike.

The Blue and the Gray

By the flow of the inland river,
    Whence the fleets of iron have fled,
Where the blades of the grave-grass quiver,
    Asleep are the ranks of the dead:
        Under the sod and the dew,
            Waiting the judgment day;
        Under the one, the Blue,
            Under the other, the Gray.

These in the robings of glory,
    Those in the gloom of defeat,
All with the battle-blood gory,
    In the dusk of eternity meet:
        Under the sod and the dew,
            Waiting the judgment day;
        Under the laurel, the Blue,
            Under the willow, the Gray.

From the silence of sorrowful hours
    The desolate mourners go,
Lovingly laden with flowers
    Alike for the friend and the foe:
        Under the sod and the dew,
            Waiting the judgment day;
        Under the roses, the Blue,
            Under the lilies, the Gray.

So with an equal splendor,
    The morning sun-rays fall,
With a touch impartially tender,
    On the blossoms blooming for all:
        Under the sod and the dew,
            Waiting the judgment day;
        Broidered with gold, the Blue,
            Mellowed with gold, the Gray.

So, when the summer calleth,
On forest and field of grain,
With an equal murmur falleth
The cooling drip of the rain:
Under the sod and the dew,
Waiting the judgment day;
Wet with the rain, the Blue,
Wet with the rain, the Gray.

Sadly, but not with upbraiding,
The generous deed was done,
In the storm of the years that are fading
No braver battle was won:
Under the sod and the dew,
Waiting the judgment day;
Under the blossoms, the Blue,
Under the garlands, the Gray.

No more shall the war cry sever,
Or the winding rivers be red;
They banish our anger forever
When they laurel the graves of our dead!
Under the sod and the dew,
Waiting the judgment day;
Love and tears for the Blue,
Tears and love for the Gray.

EDWIN MARKHAM (1852–1940). "Lincoln, the Man of the People" is among Markham's best-known poems, second in popularity only to "The Man with the Hoe."

Lincoln, the Man of the People

When the Norn-Mother saw the Whirlwind Hour,
Greatening and darkening as it hurried on,
She bent the strenuous heavens and came down
To make a man to meet the mortal need.
She took the tried clay of the common road—
Clay warm yet with the genial heat of Earth,
Dashed through it all a strain of prophecy;

Then mixed a laughter with the serious stuff.
It was a stuff to wear for centuries,
A man that matched the mountains, and compelled
The stars to look our way and honor us.

The color of the ground was in him, the red earth;
The tang and odor of the primal things—
The rectitude and patience of the rocks;
The gladness of the wind that shakes the corn;
The courage of the bird that dares the sea;
The justice of the rain that loves all leaves;
The pity of the snow that hides all scars;
The loving kindness of the wayside well;
The tolerance and equity of light
That gives as freely to the shrinking weed
As to the great oak flaring to the wind—
To the grove's low hill as to the Matterhorn
That shoulders out the sky.

                              And so he came
From prairie cabin up to Capitol,
One fair Ideal led our chieftain on.
Forevermore he burned to do his deed
With the fine stroke and gesture of a king.
He built the rail-pile as he built the State,
Pouring his splendid strength through every blow,
The conscience of him testing every stroke,
To make his deed the measure of a man.

So came the Captain with a mighty heart:
And when the step of Earthquake shook the house,
Wrenching the rafters from their ancient hold,
He held the ridgepole up, and spiked again
The rafters of the Home. He held his place—
Held the long purpose like a growing tree—
Held on through blame and faltered not at praise.
And when he fell in whirlwind, he went down
As when a kingly cedar green with boughs
Goes down with a great shout upon the hills,
And leaves a lonesome place against the sky.

AMBROSE BIERCE (1842–1914?). Essayist and story writer. He fought in the Union army, saw action in many engagements, and was wounded at Kenesaw Mountain. He disappeared in Mexico (probably killed in the civil warfare there) in 1914.

The Hesitating Veteran

When I was young and full of faith
    And other fads that youngsters cherish
A cry rose as of one that saith
    With emphasis: "Help or I perish!"
'Twas heard in all the land, and men
    The sound were each to each repeating.
It made my heart beat faster then
    Than any heart can now be beating.

For the world is old and world is gray—
    Grown prudent and, I think, more witty.
She's cut her wisdom teeth, they say,
    And doesn't now go in for Pity.
Besides, the melancholy cry
    Was that of one, 'tis now conceded,
Whose plight no one beneath the sky
    Felt half so poignantly as he did.

Moreover, he was black. And yet
    That sentimental generation
With an austere compassion set
    Its face and faith to the occasion.
Then there were hate and strife to spare,
    And various hard knocks a-plenty;
And I ('twas more than my true share,
    I must confess) took five-and-twenty.

That all is over now—the reign
    Of love and trade stills all dissensions,
And the clear heavens arch again
    Above a land of peace and pensions.
The black chap—at the last we gave
    Him everything that he had cried for,
Though many white chaps in the grave
    'Twould puzzle to say what they died for.

I hope he's better off—I trust
    That his society and his master's
Are worth the price we paid, and must
    Continue paying, in disasters;
But sometimes doubts press thronging round
    ('Tis mostly when my hurts are aching)
If war for Union was a sound
    And profitable undertaking.

'Tis said they mean to take away
    The Negro's vote for he's unlettered.
'Tis true he sits in darkness day
    And night, as formerly, when fettered;
But pray observe—howe'er he vote
    To whatsoever party turning,
He'll be with gentlemen of note
    And wealth and consequence and learning.

With saints and sages on each side,
    How could a fool through lack of knowledge,
Vote wrong? If learning is no guide
    Why ought one to have been in college?
O Son of Day, O Son of Night!
    What are your preferences made of?
I know not which of you is right,
    Nor which to be the more afraid of.
The world is old and the world is bad,
    And creaks and grinds upon its axis;
And man's an ape and the gods are mad!—
    There's nothing sure, not even our taxes.
No mortal man can Truth restore,
    Or say where she is to be sought for.
I know what uniform I wore—
    O, that I knew which side I fought for!

The Death of Grant

Father! whose hard and cruel law
    Is part of thy compassion's plan,

Thy works presumptuously we scan
For what the prophets say they saw.
Unbidden still the awful slope
   Walling us in we climb to gain
   Assurance of the shining plain
That faith has certified to hope.

In vain!—beyond the circling hill
   The shadow and the cloud abide.
   Subdue the doubt, our spirits guide
To trust the record and be still.

To trust it loyally as he
   Who, heedful of his high design,
   Ne'er raised a seeking eye to thine,
But wrought thy will unconsciously,

Disputing not of chance or fate,
   Nor questioning of cause or creed;
   For anything but duty's deed
Too simply wise, too humbly great.

The cannon syllabled his name;
   His shadow shifted o'er the land,
   Portentous, as at his demand
Successive bastions sprang to flame!
He flared the continent with fire,
   The rivers ran in lines of light!
   Thy will be done on earth—if right
Or wrong he cared not to inquire.

His was the heavy hand, and his
   The service of the despot blade;
   His the soft answer that allayed
War's giant animosities.

Let us have peace: our clouded eyes,
   Fill, Father, with another light,
   That we may see with clearer sight
Thy servant's soul in Paradise.

BRET HARTE (1836–1902). Essayist, short-story writer, novelist, and poet. Most of his Civil War poems were written from 1864 to 1867, while secretary of the United States Mint in San Francisco.

The Reveille

Hark! I hear the tramp of thousands,
   And of armèd men the hum;
Lo! a nation's hosts have gathered
   Round the quick-alarming drum—
         Saying: "Come,
         Freemen, come!
Ere your heritage be wasted," said the quick-alarming drum.

"Let me of my heart take counsel:
   War is not of life the sum;
Who shall stay and reap the harvest
   When the autumn days shall come?"
         But the drum
         Echoed: "Come!
Death shall reap the braver harvest," said the solemn-sounding
   drum.

"But when won the coming battle,
   What of profit springs therefrom?
What if conquest, subjugation,
   Even greater ills become?"
         But the drum
         Answered: "Come!
You must do the sum to prove it," said the Yankee-answering drum.

"What if, 'mid the cannons' thunder,
   Whistling shot and bursting bomb,
When my brothers fall around me,
   Should my heart grow cold and numb?"
         But the drum
         Answered: "Come!
Better there in death united than in life a recreant—Come!"

Thus they answered—hoping, fearing,
   Some in faith and doubting some,
Till a trumpet-voice proclaiming,

Said: "My chosen people, come!"
   Then the drum,
    Lo! was dumb;
For the great heart of the nation, throbbing, answered: "Lord, we
  come!"

A Second Review of the Grand Army

I read last night of the Grand Review
 In Washington's chiefest avenue—
Two hundred thousand men in blue,
 I think they said was the number—
Till I seemed to hear their trampling feet,
The bugle blast and the drum's quick beat
The clatter of hoofs in the stony street,
The cheers of people who came to greet,
And the thousand details that to repeat
 Would only my verse encumber—
Till I fell in a revery, sad and sweet,
 And then to a fitful slumber.

When, lo! in a vision I seemed to stand
In the lonely Capitol. On each hand
Far stretched the portico, dim and grand
Its columns ranged, like a martial band
Of sheeted spectres, whom some command
 Had called to a last reviewing.
And the streets of the city were white and bare;
No footfall echoed across the square;
But out of the misty midnight air
I heard in the distance a trumpet blare,
And the wandering night winds seemed to bear
 The sound of a far tattooing.

Then I held my breath with fear and dread;
For into the square, with a brazen tread,
There rode a figure whose stately head
 O'erlooked the review that morning,
That never bowed from its firm set seat
When the living column passed its feet,

Yet now rode steadily up the street
   To the phantom bugle's warning:

Till it reached the Capitol square, and wheeled,
And there in the moonlight stood revealed
A well-known form that in State and field
   Had led our patriot sires:
Whose face was turned to the sleeping camp,
Afar through the river's fog and damp,
That showed no flicker, nor waning lamp,
   Nor wasted bivouac fires.

And I saw a phantom army come,
With never a sound of fife or drum,
But keeping time to a throbbing hum
   Of wailing and lamentation:
The martyred heroes of Malvern Hill,
Of Gettysburg and Chancellorsville,
The men whose wasted figures fill
   The patriot graves of the nation.

And there came the nameless dead—the men
Who perished in fever-swamp and fen,
The slowly-starved of the prison-pen;
   And, marching beside the others,
Came the dusky martyrs of Pillow's fight,
With limbs enfranchised and bearing bright:
I thought—perhaps 't was the pale moonlight—
   They looked as white as their brothers!

And so all night marched the Nation's dead,
With never a banner above them spread,
Nor a badge, nor a motto brandishèd;
No mark—save the bare uncovered head
   Of the silent bronze Reviewer;
With never an arch save the vaulted sky;
With never a flower save those that lie
On the distant graves—for love could buy
   No gift that was purer or truer.

So all night long swept the strange array;
So all night long, till the morning gray,

I watch'd for one who had passed away,
　　With a reverent awe and wonder—
Till a blue cap waved in the lengthening line,
And I knew that one who was kin of mine
Had come; and I spake—and lo! that sign
　　Awakened me from my slumber.

WALT WHITMAN (1819–1892). Inspired by the sights he saw near the front lines and his experiences caring for the wounded in Washington hospitals, Whitman's poems are without doubt the greatest of the Civil War. All of the following poems were written between 1861 and 1865.

Beat! Beat! Drums!

Beat! beat! drums!—blow! bugles! blow!
Through the windows—through doors—burst like a ruthless force,
Into the solemn church, and scatter the congregation,
Into the school where the scholar is studying;
Leave not the bridegroom quiet—no happiness must he have now
　　with his bride,
Nor the peaceful farmer any peace, ploughing his field or gathering
　　his grain,
So fierce you whirr and pound you drums—so shrill you bugles blow.

Beat! beat! drums!—blow! bugles! blow!
Over the traffic of cities—over the rumble of wheels in the streets;
Are beds prepared for sleepers at night in the houses? no sleepers
　　must sleep in those beds,
No bargainers' bargains by day—no brokers or speculators—would
　　they continue?
Would the talkers be talking? would the singer attempt to sing?
Would the lawyer rise in the court to state his case before the judge?
Then rattle quicker, heavier drums—you bugles wilder blow.

Beat! beat! drums!—blow! bugles! blow!
Make no parley—stop for no expostulation,
Mind not the timid—mind not the weeper or prayer,
Mind not the old man beseeching the young man,
Let not the child's voice be heard, nor the mother's entreaties,
Make even the trestles to shake the dead where they lie awaiting the
　　hearses,
So strong you thump O terrible drums—so loud you bugles blow.

Cavalry Crossing a Ford

A line in long array where they wind betwixt green islands,
They take a serpentine course, their arms flash in the sun—hark to
    the musical clank,
Behold the silvery river, in it the splashing horses loitering stop to
    drink,
Behold the brown-faced men, each group, each person a picture, the
    negligent rest on the saddles,
Some emerge on the opposite bank, others are just entering the ford—
    while,
Scarlet and blue and snowy white,
The guidon flags flutter gayly in the wind.

Bivouac on a Mountain Side

I see before me now a traveling army halting,
Below a fertile valley spread, with barns and the orchards of summer,
Behind, the terraced sides of a mountain, abrupt, in places rising high,
Broken, with rocks, with clinging cedars, with tall shapes dingily seen,
The numerous camp-fires scatter'd near and far, some away up on the
    mountain,
The shadowy forms of men and horses, looming, large-sized, flickering,
And over all the sky—the sky! far, far out of reach, studded, breaking
    out, the eternal stars.

An Army Corps on the March

With its cloud of skirmishers in advance,
With now the sound of a single shot snapping like a whip, and now an
    irregular volley,
The swarming ranks press on and on, the dense brigades press on,
Glittering dimly, toiling under the sun—the dust-cover'd men,
In columns rise and fall to the undulations of the ground,
With artillery interspers'd—the wheels rumble, the horses sweat,
As the army corps advances.

Vigil Strange I Kept on the Field One Night

Vigil strange I kept on the field one night;
When you my son and my comrade dropt at my side that day,
One look I but gave which your dear eyes return'd with a look I shall
    never forget,
One touch of your hand to mine O boy, reach'd up as you lay on the
    ground,
Then onward I sped in the battle, the even-contested battle,
Till late in the night reliev'd to the place at last again I made my way,
Found you in death so cold dear comrade, found your body son of
    responding kisses, (never again on earth responding,)
Bared your face in the starlight, curious the scene, cool blew the
    moderate night-wind,
Long there and then in vigil I stood, dimly around me the battlefield
    spreading,
Vigil wondrous and vigil sweet there in the fragrant silent night,
But not a tear fell, not even a long-drawn sigh, long, long I gazed,
Then on the earth partially reclining sat by your side leaning my chin
    in my hands,
Passing sweet hours, immortal and mystic hours with you dearest
    comrade—not a tear, not a word,
Vigil of silence, love and death, vigil for you my son and my soldier,
As onward silently stars aloft, eastward new ones upward stole,
Vigil final for you brave boy, (I could not save you, swift was your
    death,
I faithfully loved you and cared for you living, I think we shall surely
    meet again,)
Till at latest lingering of the night, indeed just as the dawn appear'd,
My comrade I wrapt in his blanket, envelop'd well his form,
Folded the blanket well, tucking it carefully over head and carefully
    under feet.
And there and then and bathed by the rising sun, my son in his grave,
    in his rude-dug grave I deposited,
Ending my vigil strange with that, vigil of night and battlefield dim,
Vigil for boy of responding kisses, (never again on earth responding,)
Vigil for comrade swiftly slain, vigil I never forget, how as day
    brighten'd,
I rose from the chill ground and folded my soldier well in his blanket,
And buried him where he fell.

A March in the Ranks Hard-Prest, and the Road Unknown

A march in the ranks hard-prest, and the road unknown,
A route through a heavy wood with muffled steps in the darkness,
Our army foil'd with loss severe, and the sullen remnant retreating,
Till after midnight glimmer upon us the lights of a dim-lighted
    building,
We come to an open space in the woods, and halt by the dim-lighted
    building,
'Tis a large old church at the crossing roads, now an impromptu
    hospital,
Entering but for a minute I see a sight beyond all the pictures and
    poems ever made,
Shadows of deepest, deepest black, just lit by moving candles and
    lamps,
And by one great pitchy torch stationary with wild red flame and
    clouds of smoke,
By these, crowds, groups of forms vaguely I see on the floor, some in
    the pews laid down,
At my feet more distinctly a soldier, a mere lad, in danger of bleeding
    to death, (he is shot in the abdomen,)
I stanch the blood temporarily, (the youngster's face is white as a lily,)
Then before I depart I sweep my eyes o'er the scene fain to absorb
    it all,
Faces, varieties, postures beyond description, most in obscurity, some
    of them dead,
Surgeons operating, attendants holding lights, the smell of ether, the
    odor of blood,
The crowd, O the crowd of the bloody forms, the yard outside
    also fill'd,
Some on the bare ground, some on planks or stretchers, some in the
    death-spasm sweating,
An occasional scream or cry, the doctor's shouted orders or calls,
The glisten of the little steel instruments catching the glint of the
    torches,
These I resume as I chant, I see again the forms, I smell the odor,
Then hear outside the orders given, *Fall in, my men, fall in;*
But first I bend to the dying lad, his eyes open, a half-smile gives
    he me,
Then the eyes close, calmly close, and I speed forth to the darkness,
Resuming, marching, ever in darkness marching, on in the ranks,
The unknown road still marching.

A Sight in Camp in the Daybreak Gray and Dim

A sight in camp in the daybreak gray and dim,
As from my tent I emerge so early sleepless,
As slow I walk in the cool fresh air the path near by the hospital tent,
Three forms I see on stretchers lying, brought out there untended
lying,
Over each the blanket spread, ample brownish woolen blanket,
Gray and heavy blanket, folding, covering all.

Curious I halt and silent stand,
Then with light fingers I from the face of the nearest the first just lift
the blanket;
Who are you elderly man so gaunt and grim, with well-gray'd hair, and
flesh all sunken about the eyes?
Who are you my dear comrade?
Then to the second I step—and who are you my child and darling?
Who are you sweet boy with cheeks yet blooming?

Then to the third—a face nor child nor old, very calm, as of beautiful
yellow-white ivory;
Young man I think I know you—I think this face is the face of the
Christ himself,
Dead and divine and brother of all, and here again he lies.

The Wound-Dresser

1   An old man bending I come among new faces,
Years looking backward resuming in answer to children,
Come tell us old man, as from young men and maidens that
love me,
(Arous'd and angry, I'd thought to beat the alarum, and urge
relentless war,
But soon my fingers fail'd me, my face droop'd and I resign'd
myself,
To sit by the wounded and soothe them, or silently watch the dead;)
Years hence of these scenes, of these furious passions, these chances,
Of unsurpass'd heroes, (was one side so brave? the other was
equally brave;)
Now be witness again, paint the mightiest armies of earth,
Of those armies so rapid so wondrous what saw you to tell us?

What stays with you latest and deepest? of curious panics,
Of hard-fought engagements or sieges tremendous what deepest
    remains?

2   O maidens and young men I love and that love me,
What you ask of my days those the strangest and sudden your
    talking recalls,
Soldier alert I arrive after a long march cover'd with sweat and dust,
In the nick of time I come, plunge in the fight, loudly shout in the
    rush of successful charge,
Enter the captur'd works—yet lo, like a swift running river they
    fade,
Pass and are gone they fade—I dwell not on soldiers' perils or
    soldiers' joys,
(Both I remember well—many of the hardships, few the joys, yet I
    was content.)

But in silence, in dreams' projections,
While the world of gain and appearance and mirth goes on,
So soon what is over forgotten, and waves wash the imprints off
    the sand,
With hinged knees returning I enter the doors, (while for you up
    there,
  Whoever you are, follow without noise and be of strong heart.)

Bearing the bandages, water and sponge,
Straight and swift to my wounded I go,
Where they lie on the ground after the battle brought in,
Where their priceless blood reddens the grass the ground,
Or to the rows of the hospital tent, or under the roof'd hospital,
To the long rows of cots up and down each side I return,
To each and all one after another I draw near, not one do I miss,
An attendant follows holding a tray, he carries a refuse pail,
Soon to be fill'd with clotted rags and blood, emptied, and fill'd again.

I onward go, I stop,
With hinged knees and steady hand to dress wounds,
I am firm with each, the pangs are sharp yet unavoidable,
One turns to me his appealing eyes—poor boy! I never knew you,
Yet I think I could not refuse this moment to die for you, if that
    would save you.

3   On, on I go, (open doors of time! open hospital doors!)
     The crush'd head I dress, (poor crazed hand tear not the bandage
          away,)
     The neck of the cavalry-man with the bullet through and through
          I examine,
     Hard the breathing rattles, quite glazed already the eye, yet life
          struggles hard,
     (Come sweet death! be persuaded O beautiful death!
     In mercy come quickly.)

     From the stump of the arm, the amputated hand,
     I undo the clotted lint, remove the slough, wash off the matter
          and blood,
     Back on his pillow the soldier bends with curv'd neck and side
          falling head,
     His eyes are closed, his face is pale, he dares not look on the
          bloody stump,
     And has not yet look'd on it.
     I dress a wound in the side, deep, deep,
     But a day or two more, for see the frame all wasted and sinking,
     And the yellow-blue countenance see.

     I dress the perforated shoulder, the foot with the bullet-wound,
     Cleanse the one with a gnawing and putrid gangrene, so sickening,
          so offensive,
     While the attendant stands behind aside me holding the tray and
          pail.

     I am faithful, I do not give out,
     The fractur'd thigh, the knee, the wound in the abdomen,
     These and more I dress with impassive hand, (yet deep in my breast
          a fire, a burning flame.)

4   Thus in silence in dreams' projections,
     Returning, resuming, I thread my way through the hospitals,
     The hurt and wounded I pacify with soothing hand,
     I sit by the restless all the dark night, some are so young,
     Some suffer so much, I recall the experience sweet and sad,
     Many a soldier's loving arms about this neck have cross'd and
          rested,
     Many a soldier's kiss dwells on these bearded lips.)

The Artilleryman's Vision

While my wife at my side lies slumbering, and the wars are over long,
And my head on the pillow rests at home, and the vacant midnight
    passes,
And through the stillness, through the dark, I hear, just hear, the breath
    of my infant,
There in the room as I wake from sleep this vision presses upon me;
The engagement opens there and then in fantasy unreal,
The skirmishers begin, they crawl cautiously ahead, I hear the irregular
    snap! snap!
I hear the sounds of the different missiles, the short *t-h-t! t-h-t!* of the
    rifle-balls,
I see the shells exploding leaving small white clouds, I hear the great
    shells shrieking as they pass,
The grape like the hum and whirr of wind through the trees, (tumultuous
    now the contest rages,)
All the scenes at the batteries rise in detail before me again,
The crashing and smoking, the pride of the men in their pieces,
The chief-gunner ranges and sights his piece and selects a fuse of the
    right time,
After firing I see him lean aside and look eagerly off to note the effect;
Elsewhere I hear the cry of a regiment charging, (the young colonel
    leads himself this time with brandish'd sword,)
I see the gaps cut by the enemy's volleys, (quickly fill'd up, no delay,)
I breathe the suffocating smoke, then the flat clouds hover low
    concealing all;
Now a strange lull for a few seconds, not a shot fired on either side,
Then resumed the chaos louder than ever, with eager calls and orders
    of officers
While from some distant part of the field the wind wafts to my ears a
    shout of applause, (some special success,)
And ever the sound of the cannon far or near, (rousing even in dreams
    a devilish exultation and all the old mad joy in the depths of
    my soul,)
And ever the hastening of infantry shifting positions, batteries, cavalry,
    moving hither and thither,
(The falling, dying, I heed not, the wounded dripping and red I heed
    not, some to the rear are hobbling,)
Grime, heat, rush, aides-de-camp galloping by or on a full run,

With the patter of small arms, the warning *s-s-t* of the rifles, (these in my
    vision I hear or see,)
And bombs bursting in air, and at night the vari-color'd rockets.

To a Certain Civilian

Did you ask dulcet rhymes from me?
Did you seek the civilian's peaceful and languishing rhymes?
Did you find what I sang erewhile so hard to follow?
Why I was not singing erewhile for you to follow, to understand — nor
    am I now;
(I have been born of the same as the war was born,
The drum-corps' rattle is ever to me sweet music, I love well the martial
    dirge,
With slow wail and convulsive throb leading the officer's funeral;)
What to such as you anyhow such a poet as I? therefore leave my works,
And go lull yourself with what you can understand, and with piano-
    tunes,
For I lull nobody, and you will never understand me.

O Captain! My Captain!

O Captain! my Captain! our fearful trip is done,
The ship has weather'd every rack, the prize we sought is won,
The port is near, the bells I hear, the people all exulting,
While follow eyes the steady keel, the vessel grim and daring;
        But O heart! heart! heart!
       O the bleeding drops of red,
          Where on the deck my Captain lies,
            Fallen cold and dead.

O Captain! my Captain! rise up and hear the bells;
Rise up — for you the flag is flung — for you the bugle trills,
For you bouquets and ribbon'd wreaths — for you the shores
    a-crowding,

For you they call, the swaying mass, their eager faces turning;
    Here Captain! dear father!
        The arm beneath your head!
          It is some dream that on the deck,
            You've fallen cold and dead.

My Captain does not answer, his lips are pale and still,
My father does not feel my arm, he has no pulse nor will,
The ship is anchor'd safe and sound, its voyage closed and done,
From fearful trip the victor ship comes in with object won:
    Exult O shores, and ring O bells!
      But I with mournful tread,
        Walk the deck my Captain lies,
          Fallen cold and dead.

When Lilacs Last in the Dooryard Bloom'd

1   When lilacs last in the dooryard bloom'd,
    And the great star early droop'd in the western sky in the night,
    I mourn'd, and yet shall mourn with ever-returning spring.

    Ever-returning spring, trinity sure to me you bring,
    Lilac blooming perennial and drooping star in the west,
    And thought of him I love.

2   O powerful western fallen star!
    O shades of night—O moody, tearful night!
    O great star disappear'd—O the black murk that hides the star!
    O cruel hands that hold me powerless—O helpless soul of me!
    O harsh surrounding cloud that will not free my soul.

3   In the dooryard fronting an old farm-house near the whitewash'd
      palings,
    Stands the lilac-bush tall-growing with heart-shaped leaves of rich
      green,
    With many a pointed blossom rising delicate, with the perfume strong
      I love,
    With every leaf a miracle—and from this bush in the dooryard,
    With delicate-color'd blossoms and heart-shaped leaves of rich green,
    A sprig with its flower I break.

4   In the swamp in secluded recesses,
     A shy and hidden bird is warbling a song.

     Solitary the thrush,
     The hermit withdrawn to himself, avoiding the settlements,
     Sings by himself a song.

     Song of the bleeding throat,
     Death's outlet song of life, (for well dear brother I know,
     If thou wast not granted to sing thou would'st surely die.)

5   Over the breast of the spring, the land, amid cities,
     Amid lanes and through old woods, where lately the violets peep'd from
          the ground, spotting the gray debris,
     Amid the grass in the fields each side of the lanes, passing the endless
          grass,
     Passing the yellow-spear'd wheat, every grain from its shroud in the
          dark-brown fields uprisen,
     Passing the apple-tree blows of white and pink in the orchards,
     Carrying a corpse to where it shall rest in the grave,
     Night and day journeys a coffin.

6   Coffin that passes through lanes and streets,
     Through day and night with the great cloud darkening the land,
     With the pomp of the inloop'd flags with the cities draped in black,
     With the show of the States themselves as of crape-veil'd women
          standing,
     With processions long and winding and the flambeaus of the night,
     With the countless torches lit, with the silent sea of faces and the
          unbared heads,
     With the waiting depot, the arriving coffin, and the sombre faces,
     With dirges through the night, with the thousand voices rising strong
          and solemn,
     With all the mournful voices of the dirges pour'd around the coffin,
     The dim-lit churches and the shuddering organs—where amid these
          you journey,
     With the tolling tolling bells' perpetual clang,
     Here, coffin that slowly passes,
     I give you my sprig of lilac.

7   (Nor for you, for one alone,
     Blossoms and branches green to coffins all I bring,

For fresh as the morning, thus would I chant a song for you
    O sane and sacred death.

All over bouquets of roses,
O death, I cover you over with roses and early lilies,
But mostly and now the lilac that blooms the first,
Copious I break, I break the sprigs from the bushes,
With loaded arms I come, pouring for you,
For you and the coffins all of you O death.)

8   O western orb sailing the heaven,
Now I know what you must have meant as a month since I walk'd,
As I walk'd in silence the transparent shadowy night,
As I saw you had something to tell as you bent to me night after night,
As you droop'd from the sky low down as if to my side, (while the other
    stars all look'd on,)
As we wander'd together the solemn night, (for something I know not
    what kept me from sleep,)
As the night advanced, and I saw on the rim of the west how full you
    were of woe,
As I stood on the rising ground in the breeze in the cool transparent
    night,
As I watch'd where you pass'd and was lost in the netherward black of
    the night,
As my soul in its trouble dissatisfied sank, as where you sad orb,
Concluded, dropt in the night, and was gone.

9   Sing on there in the swamp,
O singer bashful and tender, I hear your notes, I hear your call,
I hear, I come presently, I understand you,
But a moment I linger, for the lustrous star has detain'd me,
The star my departing comrade holds and detains me.

10   O how shall I warble myself for the dead one there I loved?
And how shall I deck my song for the large sweet soul that has gone?
And what shall my perfume be for the grave of him I love?

Sea-winds blown from east and west,
Blown from the Eastern sea and blown from the Western sea, till there
    on the prairies meeting,
These and with these and the breath of my chant,
I'll perfume the grave of him I love.

11   O what shall I hang on the chamber walls?
      And what shall the pictures be that I hang on the walls,
      To adorn the burial-house of him I love?

      Pictures of growing spring and farms and homes,
      With the Fourth-month eve at sundown, and the gray smoke lucid
          and bright,
      With floods of the yellow gold of the gorgeous, indolent, sinking sun,
          burning, expanding the air,
      With the fresh sweet herbage under foot, and the pale green leaves of
          the trees prolific,
      In the distance the flowing glaze, the breast of the river, with a wind-
          dapple here and there,
      With ranging hills on the banks, with many a line against the sky,
          and shadows,
      And the city at hand with dwellings so dense, and stacks of chimneys,
      And all the scenes of life and the workshops, and the workmen home-
          ward returning.

12   Lo, body and soul—this land,
      My own Manhattan with spires, and the sparkling and hurrying tides,
          and the ships,
      The varied and ample land, the South and the North in the light,
          Ohio's shores and flashing Missouri,
      And ever the far-spreading prairies cover'd with grass and corn.

      Lo, the most excellent sun so calm and haughty,
      The violet and purple morn with just-felt breezes,
      The gentle soft-born measureless light,
      The miracle spreading bathing all, the fulfill'd noon,
      The coming eve delicious, the welcome's night and the stars,
      Over my cities shining all, enveloping man and land.

13   Sing on, sing on you gray-brown bird,
      Sing from the swamps, the recesses, pour your chant from the bushes,
      Limitless out of the dusk, out of the cedars and pines.

      Sing on dearest brother, warble your reedy song,
      Loud human song, with voice of uttermost woe.

      O liquid and free and tender!
      O wild and loose to my soul—O wondrous singer!
      You only I hear—yet the star holds me, (but will soon depart,)
      Yet the lilac with mastering odor holds me.

14   Now while I sat in the day and look'd forth,
In the close of the day with its light and the fields of spring, and the
       farmers preparing their crops,
In the large unconscious scenery of my land with its lakes and forests,
In the heavenly aerial beauty, (after the perturb'd winds and
       the storms,)
Under the arching heavens of the afternoon swift passing, and the
       voices of children and women,
The many-moving sea-tides, and I saw the ships how they sail'd,
And the summer approaching with richness, and the fields all busy with
       labor,
And the infinite separate houses, how they all went on, each with its
       meals and minutia of daily usages,
And the streets how their throbbings throbb'd, and the cities
pent—lo, then and there,
Falling upon them all and among them all, enveloping me with the rest,
Appear'd the cloud, appear'd the long black trail,
And I knew death, its thought, and the sacred knowledge of death.

Then with the knowledge of death as walking one side of me,
And the thought of death close-walking the other side of me,
And I in the middle as with companions, and as holding the hands of
       companions,
I fled forth to the hiding receiving night that talks not,
Down to the shores of the water, the path by the swamp in the dimness,
To the solemn shadowy cedars and ghostly pines so still.

And the singer so shy to the rest receiv'd me,
The gray-brown bird I know receiv'd us comrades three,
And he sang the carol of death, and a verse for him I love.

From deep secluded recesses,
From the fragrant cedars and the ghostly pines so still,
Came the carol of the bird.

And the charm of the carol rapt me,
As I held as if by their hands my comrades in the night,
And the voice of my spirit tallied the song of the bird.

Come lovely and soothing death,
Undulate round the world, serenely arriving, arriving,
In the day, in the night, to all, to each,
Sooner or later delicate death.

Prais'd be the fathomless universe,
For life and joy, and for objects and knowledge curious,
And for love, sweet love—but praise! praise! praise!
For the sure-enwinding arms of cool-enfolding death.

Dark mother always gliding near with soft feet,
Have none chanted for thee a chant of fullest welcome?
Then I chant it for thee, I glorify thee above all,
I bring thee a song that when thou must indeed come, come unfalteringly.

Approach strong deliveress,
When it is so, when thou hast taken them I joyously sing the dead,
Lost in the loving floating ocean of thee,
Laved in the flood of thy bliss O death.

From me to thee glad serenades,
Dances for thee I propose saluting thee, adornments and feastings
for thee,
And the sights of the open landscape and the high-spread sky are fitting,
And life and the fields, and the huge and thoughtful night.

The night in silence under many a star,
The ocean shore and the husky whispering wave whose voice I know,
And the soul turning to thee O vast and well-veil'd death,
And the body gratefully nestling close to thee.

Over the tree-tops I float thee a song,
Over the rising and sinking waves, over the myriad fields and the prairies
wide,
Over the dense-pack'd cities all and the teeming wharves and ways,
I float this carol with joy, with joy to thee O death.

15 To the tally of my soul,
Loud and strong kept up the gray-brown bird,
With pure deliberate notes spreading filling the night.

Loud in the pines and cedars dim,
Clear in the freshness moist and the swamp-perfume,
And I with my comrades there in the night.

While my sight that was bound in my eyes unclosed,
As to long panoramas of visions.
And I saw askant the armies,
I saw as in noiseless dreams hundreds of battle-flags,
Borne through the smoke of the battles and pierc'd with missiles I
saw them,

And carried hither and yon through the smoke, and torn and bloody,
And at last but a few shreds left on the staffs, (and all in silence,)
And the staffs all splinter'd and broken.

I saw battle-corpses, myriads of them,
And the white skeletons of young men, I saw them,
I saw the debris and debris of all the slain soldiers of the war,
But I saw they were not as was thought,
They themselves were fully at rest, they suffer'd not,
The living remain'd and suffer'd, the mother suffer'd,
And the wife and the child and the musing comrade suffer'd,
And the armies that remain'd suffer'd.

16   Passing the visions, passing the night,
Passing, unloosing the hold of my comrades' hands,
Passing the song of the hermit bird and the tallying song of my soul,
Victorious song, death's outlet song, yet varying ever-altering song,
As low and wailing, yet clear the notes, rising and falling, flooding
    the night,
Sadly sinking and fainting, as warning and warning, and yet again
    bursting with joy,
Covering the earth and filling the spread of the heaven,
As that powerful psalm in the night I heard from recesses,
Passing, I leave thee lilac with heart-shaped leaves,
I leave thee there in the dooryard, blooming, returning with spring.

I cease from my song for thee,
From my gaze on thee in the west, fronting the west, communing
    with thee,
O comrade lustrous with silver face in the night.

Yet each to keep and all, retrievements out of the night,
The song, the wondrous chant of the gray-brown bird,
And the tallying chant, the echo arous'd in my soul,
With the lustrous and drooping star with the countenance full of woe,
With the holders holding my hand nearing the call of the bird,
Comrades mine and I in the midst, and their memory ever to keep, for
    the dead I loved so well,
For the sweetest, wisest soul of all my days and lands—and this for his
    dear sake,
Lilac and star and bird twined with the chant of my soul,
There in the fragrant pines and the cedars dusk and dim.

ABRAM JOSEPH RYAN (1838–1886). Ryan was a Catholic priest who served in the Confederate army as a chaplain. "The Conquered Banner" is among the most popular Confederate poems of the war.

The Conquered Banner

Furl that Banner, for 'tis weary;
Round its staff 'tis drooping dreary;
   Furl it, fold it—it is best;
For there's not a man to wave it,
And there's not a sword to save it,
And there's not one left to lave it
In the blood which heroes gave it;
And its foes now scorn and brave it;
   Furl it, hide it—let it rest!

Take that Banner down! 'tis tattered;
Broken is its staff and shattered;
And the valiant hosts are scattered,
   Over whom it floated high.
Oh, 'tis hard for us to fold it,
Hard to think there's none to hold it,
Hard that those who once unrolled it
   Now must furl it with a sigh!

Furl that Banner—furl it sadly;
Once ten thousands hailed it gladly,
And ten thousands wildly, madly,
   Swore it should forever wave—
Swore that foeman's sword should never
Hearts like theirs entwined dissever,
Till that flag should float forever
   O'er their freedom or their grave!

Furl it! for the hands that grasped it,
And the hearts that fondly clasped it,
   Cold and dead are lying low;
And that Banner—it is trailing,
While around it sounds the wailing
   Of its people in their woe.

For, though conquered, they adore it—
Love the cold, dead hands that bore it!

Weep for those who fell before it!
Pardon those who trailed and tore it!
But, oh, wildly they deplore it,
    Now who furl and fold it so!

Furl that Banner! True, 'tis gory,
Yet 'tis wreathed around with glory,
And 'twill live in song and story
    Though its folds are in the dust!
For its fame on brightest pages,
Penned by poets and by sages,
Shall go sounding down the ages—
    Furl its folds though now we must.

Furl that Banner, softly, slowly;
Treat it gently—it is holy,
    For it droops above the dead;
Touch it not—unfold it never;
Let it droop there, furled forever—
    For its people's hopes are fled.

JAMES RUSSELL LOWELL (1819–1891). Author of The Biglow Papers and A Fable for Critics. In July 1865 he was asked by Harvard University to write the official ode commemorating her alumni slain in the war. Lowell's long poem has been criticized for being abstract and rhetorical, although the section on Lincoln has always found favor.

Ode Recited at the Harvard Commemoration, July 21, 1865

I

    Weak-winged is song,
Nor aims at that clear-ethered height
Whither the brave deed climbs for light:
    We seem to do them wrong,
Bringing our robin's-leaf to deck their hearse
Who in warm life-blood wrote their nobler verse,
Our trivial song to honor those who come
With ears attuned to strenuous trump and drum,
And shaped in squadron-strophes their desire,

Live battle-odes whose lines were steel and fire:
　　Yet sometimes feathered words are strong,
A gracious memory to buoy up and save
From Lethe's dreamless ooze, the common grave
　　Of the unventurous throng.

II

Today our Reverend Mother welcomes back
　　Her wisest Scholars, those who understood
The deeper teaching of her mystic tome,
　　And offered their fresh lives to make it good:
　　　　No lore of Greece or Rome,
No science peddling with the names of things,
Or reading stars to find inglorious fates,
　　　　Can lift our life with wings
Far from Death's idle gulf that for the many waits,
　　　　And lengthen out our dates
With that clear fame whose memory sings
In manly hearts to come, and nerves them and dilates:
Nor such thy teaching, Mother of us all!
　　　　Not such the trumpet-call
　　　　Of thy diviner mood,
　　　　That could thy sons entice
From happy homes and toils, the fruitful nest
Of those half-virtues which the world calls best,
　　　　Into War's tumult rude;
　　　　But rather far that stern device
The sponsors chose that round thy cradle stood
　　　　In the dim, unventured wood,
　　　　The VERITAS that lurks beneath
　　　　The letter's unprolific sheath,
　　Life of whate'er makes life worth living,
Seed-grain of high emprise, immortal-food,
　　One heavenly thing whereof earth hath the giving.

III

Many loved Truth, and lavished life's best oil
　　Amid the dust of books to find her,
Content at last, for guerdon of their toil,
　　With the cast mantle she hath left behind her.

Many in sad faith sought for her,
Many with crossed hands sighed for her;
But these, our brothers, fought for her,
At life's dear peril wrought for her,
So loved her that they died for her,
Tasting the raptured fleetness
Of her divine completeness:
Their higher instinct knew
Those love her best who to themselves are true,
And what they dare to dream of, dare to do;
They followed her and found her
Where all may hope to find,
Not in the ashes of the burnt-out mind,
But beautiful, with danger's sweetness round her.
Where faith made whole with deed
Breathes its awakening breath
Into the lifeless creed,
They saw her plumed and mailed,
With sweet, stern face unveiled,
And all-repaying eyes, look proud on them in death.

IV

Our slender life runs rippling by, and glides
Into the silent hollow of the past;
What is there that abides
To make the next age better for the last?
Is earth too poor to give us
Something to live for here that shall outlive us?
Some more substantial boon
Than such as flows and ebbs with Fortune's fickle moon?
The little that we see
From doubt is never free;
The little that we do
Is but half-nobly true;
With our laborious hiving
What men call treasure, and the gods call dross,
Life seems a jest of Fate's contriving,
Only secure in every one's conniving,
A long account of nothings paid with loss,
Where we poor puppets, jerked by unseen wires,
After our little hour of strut and rave,
With all our pasteboard passions and desires,

Loves, hates, ambitions, and immortal fires,
　Are tossed pell-mell together in the grave.
But stay! no age was e'er degenerate,
　Unless men held it at too cheap a rate,
For in our likeness still we shape our fate.
　　Ah, there is something here
　Unfathomed by the cynic's sneer,
Something that gives our feeble light
A high immunity from Night.
Something that leaps life's narrow bars
To claim its birthright with the hosts of heaven;
　A seed of sunshine that can leaven
　Our earthy dulness with the beams of stars
　　　And glorify our clay
　With light from fountains elder than the Day;
　A conscience more divine than we,
　A gladness fed with secret tears,
　A vexing, forward-reaching sense
　Of some more noble permanence;
　　　A light across the sea,
Which haunts the soul and will not let it be,
Still beaconing from the heights of undegenerate years.

V

　　　Wither leads the path
　　　To ampler fates that leads?
　　　Not down through flowery meads,
　　　To reap an aftermath
　　Of youth's vainglorious weeds,
　　But up the steep, amid the wrath
And shock of deadly-hostile creeds,
　Where the world's best hope and stay
By battle's flashes gropes a desperate way,
And every turf the fierce foot clings to bleeds.
　Peace hath her not ignoble wreath,
　Ere yet the sharp, decisive word
Light the black lips of cannon, and the sword
　　Dreams in its easeful sheath;
But some day the live coal behind the thought,
　　Whether from Baäl's stone obscene,
　　Or from the shrine serene
　　Of God's pure altar brought,

Bursts up in flame; the war of tongue and pen
Learns with what deadly purpose it was fraught,
And, helpless in the fiery passion caught,
Shakes all the pillared state with shock of men:
Some day the soft Ideal that we wooed
Confronts us fiercely, foe-beset, pursued,
And cries reproachful: "Was it, then, my praise,
And not myself was loved? Prove now thy truth;
I claim of thee the promise of thy youth;
Give me thy life, or cower in empty phrase,
The victim of thy genius, not its mate!"
    Life may be given in many ways,
    And loyalty to Truth be sealed
As bravely in the closet as the field,
        So bountiful is Fate;
        But then to stand beside her,
        When craven churls deride her,
To front a lie in arms and not to yield,
        This shows, methinks, God's plan
        And measure of a stalwart man,
        Limbed like the old heroic breeds,
        Who stands self-poised on manhood's solid earth,
    Not forced to frame excuses for his birth,
Fed from within with all the strength he needs.

VI

Such was he, our Martyr-Chief,
    Whom late the Nation he had led,
    With ashes on her head,
Wept with the passion of an angry grief:
Forgive me, if from present things I turn
To speak what in my heart will beat and burn,
And hang my wreath on his world-honored urn.
    Nature, they say, doth dote,
    And cannot make a man
    Save on some worn-out plan,
    Repeating us by rote:
For him her Old-World moulds aside she threw,
    And, choosing sweet clay from the breast
    Of the unexhausted West,

With stuff untainted shaped a hero new,
Wise, steadfast in the strength of God, and true
    How beautiful to see
Once more a shepherd of mankind indeed,
Who loved his charge, but never loved to lead;
One whose meek flock the people joyed to be,
    Not lured by any cheat of birth,
    But by his clear-grained human worth,
And brave old wisdom of sincerity!
    They knew that outward grace is dust;
    They could not choose but trust
In that sure-footed mind's unfaltering skill,
    And supple-tempered will
That bent like perfect steel to spring again and thrust.
    His was no lonely mountain-peak of mind
    Thrusting to thin air o'er our cloudy bars,
    A sea-mark now, now lost in vapors blind;
    Broad prairie rather, genial, level-lined,
    Fruitful and friendly for all human kind,
Yet also nigh to heaven and loved of loftiest stars,
        Nothing of Europe here,
Or, then, of Europe fronting mornward still,
    Ere any names of Serf and Peer
    Could Nature's equal scheme deface
    And thwart her genial will;
    Here was a type of the true elder race,
And one of Plutarch's men talked with us face to face.
    I praise him not; it were too late;
And some innative weakness there must be
In him who condescends to victory
Such as the Present gives, and cannot wait,
    Safe in himself as in a fate.
        So always firmly he:
        He knew to bide his time,
        And can his fame abide,
Still patient in his simple faith sublime,
        Till the wise years decide.
  Great captains, with their guns and drums,
    Disturb our judgment for the hour,
        But at last silence comes;

These all are gone, and, standing like a tower,
Our children shall behold his fame,
    The kindly-earnest, brave, forseeing man,
Sagacious, patient, dreading praise, not blame,
    New birth of our new soil, the first American.

VII

Long as man's hope insatiate can discern
        Or only guess some more inspiring goal
        Outside of Self, enduring as the pole,
Along whose course the flying axles burn
Of spirits bravely-pitched, earth's manlier brood;
        Long as below we cannot find
    The meed that stills the inexorable mind;
    So long this faith to some ideal Good,
    Under whatever mortal names it masks,
    Freedom, Law, Country, this ethereal mood
That thanks the Fates for their severer tasks,
    Feeling its challenged pulses leap,
    While others skulk in subterfuges cheap,
And, set in Danger's van, has all the boon it asks,
    Shall win man's praise and woman's love,
    Shall be a wisdom that we set above
All other skills and gifts to culture dear,
    A virtue round whose forehead we inwreathe
    Laurels that with a living passion breathe
When other crowns grow, while we twine them, sear.
    What brings us thronging these high rites to pay,
And seal these hours the noblest of our year,
    Save that our brothers found this better way?

VIII

We sit here in the Promised Land
That flows with Freedom's honey and milk;
But 't was they won it, sword in hand,
Making the nettle danger soft for us as silk.
    We welcome back our bravest and our best;
    Ah me! not all! some come not with the rest,
Who went forth brave and bright as any here!

I strive to mix some gladness with my strain,
   But the sad strings complain,
   And will not please the ear:
I sweep them for a pæan, but they wane
   Again and yet again
Into a dirge, and die away, in pain.
In these brave ranks I only see the gaps,
Thinking of dear ones whom the dumb turf wraps,
Dark to the triumph which they died to gain:
   Fitlier may others greet the living,
   For me the past is unforgiving;
    I with uncovered head
    Salute the sacred dead,
Who went, and who return not. — Say not so!
'T is not the grapes of Canaan that repay,
But the high faith that failed not by the way;
Virtue treads paths that end not in the grave;
No ban of endless night exiles the brave;
    And to the saner mind
We rather seem the dead that stayed behind.
Blow, trumpets, all your exultations blow!
For never shall their aureoled presence lack;
I see them muster in a gleaming row,
With ever-youthful brows that nobler show;
We find in our dull road their shining track;
    In every nobler mood
We feel the orient of their spirit glow,
Part of our life's unalterable good,
Of all our saintlier aspiration;
    They come transfigured back,
Secure from change in their high-hearted ways,
Beautiful evermore, and with the rays
Of morn on their white Shields of Expectation!

IX

   But is there hope to save
  Even this ethereal essence from the grave?
  What ever 'scaped Oblivion's subtle wrong
Save a few clarion names, or golden threads of song?

Before my musing eye
    The mighty ones of old sweep by,
Disvoicèd now and insubstantial things,
As noisy once as we; poor ghosts of kings,
Shadows of empire wholly gone to dust,
And many races, nameless long ago,
To darkness driven by that imperious gust
Of ever-rushing Time that here doth blow:
O visionary world, condition strange,
Where naught abiding is but only Change,
Where the deep-bolted stars themselves still shift and range!
        Shall we to more continuance make pretence?
Renown builds tombs; a life-estate is Wit;
                And, bit by bit,
The cunning years steal all from us but woe;
    Leaves are we, whose decays no harvest sow.
            But, when we vanish hence,
    Shall they lie forceless in the dark below,
    Save to make green their little length of sods,
    Or deepen pansies for a year or two,
    Who now to us are shining-sweet as gods?
    Was dying all they had the skill to do?
    That were not fruitless: but the Soul resents
    Such short-lived service, as if blind events
    Ruled without her, or earth could so endure;
    She claims a more divine investiture
    Of longer tenure than Fame's airy rents;
Whate'er she touches doth her nature share;
Her inspiration haunts the ennobled air,
            Gives eyes to mountains blind,
Ears to the deaf earth, voices to the wind,
And her clear trump sings succor everywhere
By lonely bivouacs to the wakeful mind;
For soul inherits all that soul could dare:
            Yea, Manhood hath a wider span
And larger privilege of life than man.
The single deed, the private sacrifice,
So radiant now through proudly-hidden tears,
Is covered up erelong from mortal eyes
With thoughtless drift of the deciduous years;
But that high privilege that makes all men peers,

That leap of heart whereby a people rise
Up to a noble anger's height,
And, flamed on by the Fates, not shrink, but grow more bright,
That swift validity in noble veins,
Of choosing danger and disdaining shame,
Of being set on flame
By the pure fire that flies all contact base,
But wraps its chosen with angelic might,
These are imperishable gains,
Sure as the sun, medicinal as light,
These hold great futures in their lusty reins
And certify to earth a new imperial race.

X

Who now shall sneer?
Who dare again to say we trace
Our lines to a plebeian race?
Roundhead and Cavalier!
Dumb are those names erewhile in battle loud;
Dream-footed as the shadow of a cloud,
They flit across the ear:
That is best blood that hath most iron in 't.
To edge resolve with, pouring without stint
For what makes manhood dear.
Tell us not of Plantagenets,
Hapsburgs, and Guelfs, whose thin bloods crawl
Down from some victor in a border-brawl!
How poor their outworn coronets,
Matched with one leaf of that plain civic wreath
Our brave for honor's blazon shall bequeath,
Through whose desert a rescued Nation sets
Her heel on treason, and the trumpet hears
Shout victory, tingling Europe's sullen ears
With vain resentments and more vain regrets!

XI

Not in anger, not in pride,
Pure from passion's mixture rude
Ever to base earth allied,
But with far-heard gratitude,

Still with heart and voice renewed,
To heroes living and dear martyrs dead,
The strain should close that consecrates our brave.
    Lift the heart and lift the head!
        Lofty be its mood and grave,
        Not without a martial ring,
        Not without a prouder tread
        And a peal of exultation:
        Little right has he to sing
        Through whose heart in such an hour
Beats no march of conscious power,
Sweeps no tumult of elation!
'T is no Man we celebrate,
By his country's victories great,
    A hero half, and half the whim of Fate,
        But the pith and marrow of a Nation
        Drawing force from all her men,
        Highest, humblest, weakest, all,
        For her time of need, and then
        Pulsing it again through them,
    Till the basest can no longer cower,
    Feeling his soul spring up divinely tall,
    Touched but in passing by her mantle-hem.
    Come back, then, noble pride, for 't is her dower!
        How could poet ever tower,
        If his passions, hopes, and fears,
        If his triumphs and his tears,
        Kept not measure with his people?
Boom, cannon, boom to all the winds and waves!
Clash out, glad bells, from every rocking steeple!
Banners, adance with triumph, bend your staves!
        And from every mountain-peak,
        Let beacon-fire to answering beacon speak,
        Katahdin tell Monadnock, Whiteface he,
And so leap on in light from sea to sea,
                Till the glad news be sent
                Across a kindling continent,
Making earth feel more firm and air breathe braver:
"Be proud! for she is saved, and all have helped to save her!
    She that lifts up the manhood of the poor,
    She of the open soul and open door,

With room about her hearth for all mankind!
The fire is dreadful in her eyes no more;
From her bold front the helm she doth unbind,
Sends all her handmaid armies back to spin,
And bids her navies, that so lately hurled
Their crashing battle, hold their thunders in,
Swimming like birds of calm along the unharmful shore.
No challenge sends she to the elder world,
That looked askance and hated; a light scorn
Plays o'er her mouth, as round her mighty knees
She calls her children back, and waits the morn
Of nobler day, enthroned between her subject seas."

XII

Bow down, dear Land, for thou hast found release!
   Thy God, in these distempered days,
   Hath taught thee the sure wisdom of His ways,
And through thine enemies hath wrought thy peace!
     Bow down in prayer and praise!
No poorest in thy borders but may now
Lift to the juster skies a man's enfranchised brow.
O Beautiful! my Country! ours once more!
Smoothing thy gold of war-dishevelled hair
O'er such sweet brows as never other wore,
     And letting thy set lips,
     Freed from wrath's pale eclipse,
The rosy edges of their smile lay bare,
What words divine of lover or of poet
Could tell our love and make thee know it,
Among the Nations bright beyond compare?
     What were our lives without thee?
     What all our lives to save thee?
     We reck not what we gave thee;
     We will not dare to doubt thee,
But ask whatever else, and we will dare!

KATE PUTNAM OSGOOD (1841–1910). In contrast to Lowell's ornately rhetorical *Ode*, Osgood's gentle poem treats the war's terrible losses in the most basic human terms.

Driving Home the Cows

Out of the clover and blue-eyed grass,
    He turned them into the river-lane;
One after another he let them pass,
    Then fastened the meadow-bars again.
Under the willows, and over the hill,
    He patiently followed their sober pace;
The merry whistle for once was still,
    And something shadowed the sunny face.

Only a boy! and his father had said
    He never could let his youngest go:
Two already were lying dead
    Under the feet of the trampling foe.

But after the evening work was done,
    And the frogs were loud in the meadow-swamp,
Over his shoulder he slung his gun,
    And stealthily followed the foot-path damp,

Across the clover, and through the wheat,
    With resolute heart and purpose grim,
Though cold was the dew on his hurrying feet,
    And the blind bat's flitting startled him.

Thrice since then had the lanes been white,
    And the orchards sweet with apple-bloom;
And now, when the cows came back at night,
    The feeble father drove them home.

For news had come to the lonely farm
    That three were lying where two had lain;
And the old man's tremulous, palsied arm
    Could never lean on a son's again.

The summer day grew cold and late.
    He went for the cows when the work was done;

But down the lane, as he opened the gate,
    He saw them coming, one by one—

Brindle, Ebony, Speckle, and Bess,
    Shaking their horns in the evening wind;
Cropping the buttercups out of the grass—
    But who was it following close behind?

Loosely swung in the idle air
    The empty sleeve of army blue;
And worn and pale, from the crisping hair,
    Looked out a face that the father knew.

For Southern prisons will sometimes yawn,
    And yield their dead unto life again;
And the day that comes with a cloudy dawn
    In golden glory at last may wane.

The great tears sprang to their meeting eyes;
    For the heart must speak when the lips are dumb;
And under the silent evening skies,
    Together they followed the cattle home.

Index of Authors and Titles

DOVER · THRIFT · EDITIONS

POETRY

THE CONGO AND OTHER POEMS, Vachel Lindsay. 96pp. 27272-9

EVANGELINE AND OTHER POEMS, Henry Wadsworth Longfellow. 64pp. 28255-4

FAVORITE POEMS, Henry Wadsworth Longfellow. 96pp. 27273-7

"TO HIS COY MISTRESS" AND OTHER POEMS, Andrew Marvell. 64pp. 29544-3

SPOON RIVER ANTHOLOGY, Edgar Lee Masters. 144pp. 27275-3

SELECTED POEMS, Claude McKay. 80pp. 40876-0

RENASCENCE AND OTHER POEMS, Edna St. Vincent Millay. 64pp. (Not available in Europe or the United Kingdom) 26873-X

FIRST FIG AND OTHER POEMS, Edna St. Vincent Millay. 80pp. (Not available in Europe or the United Kingdom) 41104-4

SELECTED POEMS, John Milton. 128pp. 27554-X

CIVIL WAR POETRY: An Anthology, Paul Negri (ed.). 128pp. 29883-3

ENGLISH VICTORIAN POETRY: AN ANTHOLOGY, Paul Negri (ed.). 256pp. 40425-0

GREAT SONNETS, Paul Negri (ed.). 96pp. 28052-7

THE RAVEN AND OTHER FAVORITE POEMS, Edgar Allan Poe. 64pp. 26685-0

ESSAY ON MAN AND OTHER POEMS, Alexander Pope. 128pp. 28053-5

GOBLIN MARKET AND OTHER POEMS, Christina Rossetti. 64pp. 28055-1

CHICAGO POEMS, Carl Sandburg. 80pp. 28057-8

CORNHUSKERS, Carl Sandburg. 157pp. 41409-4

THE SHOOTING OF DAN MCGREW AND OTHER POEMS, Robert Service. 96pp. (Available in U.S. only.) 27556-6

COMPLETE SONNETS, William Shakespeare. 80pp. 26686-9

SELECTED POEMS, Percy Bysshe Shelley. 128pp. 27558-2

AFRICAN-AMERICAN POETRY: An Anthology, 1773–1930, Joan R. Sherman (ed.). 96pp. 29604-0

NATIVE AMERICAN SONGS AND POEMS: An Anthology, Brian Swann (ed.). 64pp. 29450-1

SELECTED POEMS, Alfred Lord Tennyson. 112pp. 27282-6

AENEID, Vergil (Publius Vergilius Maro). 256pp. 28749-1

GREAT LOVE POEMS, Shane Weller (ed.). 128pp. 27284-2

CIVIL WAR POETRY AND PROSE, Walt Whitman. 96pp. 28507-3

SELECTED POEMS, Walt Whitman. 128pp. 26878-0

THE BALLAD OF READING GAOL AND OTHER POEMS, Oscar Wilde. 64pp. 27072-6

EARLY POEMS, William Carlos Williams. 64pp. (Available in U.S. only.) 29294-0

FAVORITE POEMS, William Wordsworth. 80pp. 27073-4

EARLY POEMS, William Butler Yeats. 128pp. 27808-5